PUBLICATIONS IN LIBRARIANSHIP 63

Decision-Making in the Absence of Certainty

A Study in the Context of Technology and the Construction of 21st Century Academic Libraries

by S. David Mash

Association of College and Research Libraries
A division of the American Library Association
Chicago, Illinois 2010

The paper used in this publication meets the minimum requirements of American National Standard for Information Sciences–Permanence of Paper for Printed Library Materials, ANSI Z39.48-1992. ∞

Library of Congress Cataloging-in-Publication Data

Mash, S. David (Samuel David)
  Decision-making in the absence of certainty : a study in the context of technology and the construction of 21st century academic libraries / S. David Mash.
      pages cm. -- (ACRL publications in librarianship ; no. 63)
  Includes bibliographical references.
  ISBN 978-0-8389-8571-7 (pbk. : alk. paper) 1. Library buildings--United States--Design and construction. 2. Library buildings--United States--Planning. 3. Academic libraries--Information technology--United States. 4. Academic libraries--Administration--Decision making. 5. Academic libraries--United States--Case studies. I. Title.
  Z679.2.U54M37 2010
  022'.3170973--dc22
                                    2010049544

Printed in the United States of America.

14 13 12 11 10   5 4 3 2 1

Table of Contents

Tables and Figures

Acknowledgements

This book is based on my dissertation, written during doctoral studies in higher education administration at the University of South Carolina. I owe an ongoing debt of gratitude to my dissertation committee. Michelle Maher, Katherine Chaddock, Mike Welsh, and the late Bob Skinder lead me through a process of research that actually changed the way I think about decision making. Thanks, again, to each of you.

Thanks also to the many professionals who participated in the interviews for this research. Thank you all for your generous spirit and for trusting me as you spoke so freely and with great candor. You will remain unnamed, but I will not forget you!

Finally, the unusually perceptive and expert assistance from Craig Gibson, the chair of the editorial board, has been an encouraging and rewarding. Working with Craig as he coached me through the process has made me a better writer. Thanks Craig!

for Mom and Dad

Libraries With Walls for the 21st Century

In 1927, The H.W. Wilson Company published a volume titled *The Library Without the Walls*.[1] This was not a volume of prescient thoughts on a future day when library buildings would no longer be needed. Instead, "without" was used in a now secondary sense of the term, meaning "outside" or "beyond." The editor, Laura M. Janzow of the St. Louis Public Library, brought together numerous late 19th and early 20th articles related to initiatives in library services offered beyond the library building. Examples included traveling libraries, home delivery to library users, interlibrary loans, and library services to prisoners.

In 1981, visionary librarian Wilfred Lancaster of the graduate school of library science at the University of Illinois at Urbana-Champaign delivered a paper on library automation titled *The Library Without Walls*.[2] This time "without" was taken in the now popular sense of "absence" or "lacking." The title of his paper became a catch phrase used to evoke visions of barrier free access to unlimited digital information. The print prison would give way to electronic liberation. Bits would replace books and bricks and our perennial space problems would vanish. Some, like World Bank librarian Sylvia Piggott, carried the idea a little further: "We will not be far into the 21st century before the librarian's role in the information retrieval process disappears in the face of perfected end user access."[3] Libraries without walls became—in the minds of some—libraries that also lacked books, buildings, and librarians.

But now, a decade into the 21st century, print remains a vital technology for information transfer and preservation[4] and librarians have not disappeared. The promise of electronic "perfected end user access" remains as elusive as ever, too often giving way to "access without focus, information without knowledge, choice without context, directionless and ubiquitous as the sea."[5] Library buildings continue to rise and librarianship, though different in many ways, remains a keystone profession in information services.

The idea of a library without walls is perhaps too reductionistic—too simplistic—and too easily expropriated for purposes unrelated to the vision of improved service. A more imaginative vision will account for "the importance of the library as place while simultaneously using every means to reach beyond its walls… The future library needs to move beyond walls, not dispense with walls. The future means a library that is both edifice and interface."[6]

This book is about the decision making process at five American universities that built new libraries at the dawn of the 21st century. Their collective decision to invest many millions of dollars in technology *and* physical space is a testament to their perceptive commitment to a vision that the very best for students and faculty is a library with and without the walls.

This book is not, however, an exegesis of decision making technique, a distillation of methods, or a popular account of how the experts get things done. Instead, it goes beyond technique to an exploration of hard realities that belie many of our ingrained assumptions about what decision making is and how decisions are made… or not made. Consider, for instance, the difference between examining a terrain map and actually backpacking in the wilderness. The best insight into the latter can only come through thoughtful conversation with recent wilderness backpackers.

This book explores the dynamics of decision making in higher education—with special attention to the matter of technology forecasting—as applied to the process of planning and building academic library buildings. This is done through recorded conversations with a wide range of professionals having recent "hiking" experience in the realm of library construction. The result is not an overview of methods but something much more crucial: insight into the variegated terrain of high consequence decision making in complex institutional settings. This insight will serve as a foundation for gaining and holding both professional and personal bearings in the midst of settings that can challenge both to the core.

In **Chapter 1** we see that libraries and technology have a long history of symbiosis. But initial adoption patterns, long term diffusion, and the bearing these have on the lasting significance of a new technology are phenomena that can only be described in hindsight, not predicted or controlled through foresight.

Chapter 2 describes how institutional decision making is rarely a straightforward transaction. An oversimplified interpretation of the process can prevent the kind of insight needed for fruitful progress. This is especially true in high consequence decision situations such as building programs and large scale technology purchasing.

Decision making involves making assumptions about the future (**Chapter 3**). Technology advocates speak with confidence about technology and its place in the future. But technology forecasting has an unusually weak history of success, weaker than even most advocates know. This has implications for how forecasts are used in decision making.

Chapters 4, 5, and **6** detail the findings for the central question of this research: How did library directors and other key decision making participants describe decision making—including the use of technology forecasts—during the construction of new academic libraries?

The **Conclusion** reflects on the finding that the decision making described in this research was often messy and painful. The stock portrayal of planning and decision making as deliberative engagement of a manageably stable—though perhaps unruly—environment is usurped by a picture of reflexive heuristics in an unpredictably fluid environment. Yet within the complexity, unpredictability, and uncontrollability of institutional decision settings, general patterns can be discerned, opportunities may be realized, and meaningful progress is possible. Examples and, finally, a few guiding suggestions are provided.

Notes

1. Janzow, *The Library Without the Walls: Reprints of Papers and Addresses.*
2. Lancaster, "The Library Without Walls."
3. Piggott, "The Virtual Library : Almost There…, 206.
4. See, for instance, Darnton, *The Case for Books: Past, Present, and Future* and Powers, *Hamlet's Blackberry: A Practical Philosophy for Building a Good Life in the Digital Age.*
5. Wisner, *Whither the Postmodern Library?: Libraries, Technology, and Education in the Information Age,* 55.
6. Crawford and Gorman, *Future Libraries: Dreams, Madness, & Reality,* 181.

CHAPTER ONE

Libraries, Technology, and Visions of the Future

Libraries and technology have a long history of symbiosis. But initial adoption patterns, long term diffusion, and the bearing these have on the lasting significance of a new technology are phenomena that can only be described in hindsight, not predicted or controlled through foresight.

Introduction

Working in Ephesus near the end of the sixth century B.C., Heraclitus observed that "Everything flows and nothing abides; everything gives way and nothing stays fixed."[1] This element of the human condition is perhaps the impetus for a yearning to know what lays ahead, what change will usher into life. In Rome nearly half of a millennium later, during the first century B.C., Cicero wrote that he was "aware of no people, however refined and learned or however savage and ignorant, which does not think that signs are given of future events, and that certain persons can recognize those signs and foretell events before they occur."[2] To foretell the future is to master the wake of change.

As in ancient Greece and Rome, so in America today. Following his visit to the United States in the early nineteenth century, the French politician Tocqueville noted that "democratic peoples do not bother at all about the past but they gladly start dreaming about the future, and in that direction their imagination knows no bounds, but spreads and grows beyond measure…. Democracy shuts the past… but opens the future."[3] Historian Zachary Karabell described the United States as a uniquely "visionary nation" where a belief in the "promise of a better world" is a cultural trait with both religious and secular manifestations.[4] This cultural trait has produced a "future-think industry" dating from the 1890s[5] that now draws billions in revenue each year.[6]

Harvard business professor Steven C. Wheelwright and Spyros G. Makridakis, founding editor of the *Journal of Forecasting*, highlight the relationship between prediction and decision making: "A key aspect of any decision making situation is being able to predict the circumstances that surround that decision and that situation."[7] Forecasting has been applied to libraries to predict everything from their imminent demise to the dawning of a new era. The use of technology in an increasingly diffuse set of library activities has engendered a body of literature devoted to forecasts made in relation to technological developments and how they should affect library related decision making.

Decision making related to technology adoption is, however, exceedingly complex and the sustainability of any single innovation is entirely unpredictable. One of the most prominent scholarly treatments of technology adoption is the work of University of New Mexico communications professor Everett M. Rogers. In his book *Diffusion of Innovations*, now in its fifth edition, Rogers notes that "more than just a beneficial innovation is necessary for its diffusion and adoption to occur."[8] The role of perception is central: "Innovations that are *perceived* by individuals as having greater relative advantage, compatibility, trialability, observability, and less complexity will be adopted more rapidly than other innovations."[9] Yet perceptions across pools of potential adopters are never uniform. Perception can be a function of multiple variables including personality, exposure to advertising, previous experience with similar technology, promotion by influential advocates, and whether the technology serves ancillary agendas. Even after the initial adoption of a new technology, perception remains in flux due to "anticipated versus unanticipated consequences" that accrue to the use of the technology.[10] Initial adoption patterns, long term diffusion, and the bearing these have on the lasting significance of a new technology are phenomena that can be described in hindsight but not predicted or controlled through foresight.

Yet the impulse to predict persists. Science librarians Gregg Sapp and Ron Gilmour observed that

> Throughout the latter half of the twentieth century, and especially over its last twenty-five or so years, librarians could see that much, if not everything about libraries would change. The social, economic, political,

and (perhaps above all) technological forces driving change were omnipresent and unstoppable. What was unknown, however, is exactly how and in what ways the institutions of libraries would be changed. This uncertainty was the source of both great hope and great concern. In response to these situations, there arose within the professional literature of librarianship a body of speculative and conjectural writings that attempted to analyze current conditions and to anticipate or plan for the future.[11]

A federated Boolean query of Academic Search Premier, ERIC, and Library and Information Science Abstracts, produces more than 12,000 items related to technology oriented forecasts for libraries.[12] Publications on this topic appear as early as 1950. Publication volume, however, is heavily skewed toward the most recent twenty years.[13] The same search on the OCLC WorldCat database yields over 2,000 items with a balance of nearly eighty percent favoring the most recent twenty years.[14] Overall, subjects treated in the context of technology forecasts for libraries include every conceivable aspect of library operations. The themes of "rapid," "emergent," "discontinuous," and "disruptive" permeate the terms and tone of many forecasts, rousing at times a sense of urgency, even of crisis.

Libraries and Technology

Alphabetization—originating in the third century b.c. library at Alexandria—and arcane devices such as the twelfth century binary classification scheme of Arab librarian Al'deneb, the sixteenth century French book wheel, the nineteenth century Cotgreave Indicator in England and the Rudolph Continuous Indexer represent technologies introduced by librarians in the pursuit of greater efficiency.[15]

The literature of the library profession from the late nineteenth and early twentieth centuries documents the use of a variety of technologies by librarians in the service of library operations. In 1877 Justin Winsor, once the library director at Harvard, discussed the matter of telephones in libraries[16] and in 1879, *Library Journal* published an article on the use of electric light in the British Museum reading room.[17] By 1912, a book on the construction of library buildings observed that "the use of electricity has become so general all over the country, even in small towns, the light is so good, so safe, and considering the advantages, so cheap that you are likely to arrive soon at the electrical stage."[18] This "electrical stage" would eventually lead to the suggestion, in 1936, that public libraries should "have the words 'Public Library' in neon lights high up on the roof" in order to identify the building from a distance.[19]

In 1891, an article in the journal *Library* described the typewriter as a "cataloguing appliance"[20] and by 1907 *Library Journal* noted that

> The use of the typewriter for cataloging purposes is becoming so common that some knowledge of the subject is desirable. Many librarians want applicants for positions who know how to use the machine.[21]

Yale University's use of the teleautograph drew the attention of the American Library Association in 1909.[22] The next year, vacuum cleaners made it on to *Library Journal's* list of "labor-savers in library service"[23] and in 1912 a book on how to plan library buildings concluded that "vacuum cleaners are here to stay."[24] Articles on various methods of duplication were published in library literature as early as 1877[25] and in 1916 the *ALA Bulletin* included a discussion of photographic copying in relation to library research work.[26] Very early mention of a computing device in library work appeared in a 1914 issue of *Public Libraries* as an article on a mechanical device for calculating overdue fines.[27] In 1927 a teletype machine was used for "internal communication between the stacks and the circulation desk" at The Free Library of Philadelphia[28] and by the late 1930s, libraries used automated punched-card equipment for circulation and acquisitions functions.[29]

Furthermore, libraries have promoted alternate information formats created with new technologies for more than a century. In 1899, *Library Journal* printed an article on the photograph collection at the Pratt Institute library.[30] Lantern slides and stereographs were included in library collections at least as early as 1903[31] and 1919[32] respectively. The use of "moving pictures" was treated in a 1910 *Wilson Library Bulletin* article[33] and the Victrola[34], player piano rolls[35], gramophones[36], and phonograph records[37] each had a place in pre-1920 libraries.

In 1939, a publication from the University of North Carolina emphasized that library service is much more than "the mere preservation and loan of books and magazines" and should include providing access to the technology of phonograph records.[38] Also in 1939, a publication from the American Library Association noted that "talking books" on phonograph records were provided for circulation to blind people by many libraries.[39] An early note of caution, however, was voiced by the legendary librarian and information science scholar Jesse H. Shera in 1939; he noted "the utter futility of any attempt to view library horizons merely as expanding technology."[40]

Alternate means of information delivery date from the late nineteenth century as well. In 1893, Melville Dewey, the state librarian of New York, launched a program of traveling libraries so that people in remote locations could access the content of libraries.[41] In 1901 he wrote that

> Libraries must be mobilized. Books must travel more…. The cheapness and quickness of modern methods of communication has been like a growth of wings so that a thousand things which were thought to belong like trees in one place may travel about like birds.[42]

In 1936 one author suggested the "amalgamation" of individual library collections through "the linking up" various libraries "by the telephone and transport services."[43] The philosophical disposition that made these ideas possible is the same disposition undergirding the contemporary development of bookmobiles, interlibrary loan, and the use of computer networks to deliver vetted content to remote locations.

In 1927, the director of the Newark Public Library John C. Dana wrote an article titled *Changes in Library Methods in a Changing World.*[44] He urged librarians to accept the maxim "don't worship the library, but fit it to its new job"[45] and his proposal for the use of technology articulated the now ubiquitous "access versus ownership" debate:

> Mail, telephone, wireless, photostat and television all point to the day when a librarian will be proud to say that he has thought more of giving access to all the print his patrons may need than of merely acquiring as many books as his friends will buy; and that, with funds not spent for books, he can pay for bringing a needed book

to his library or can get photos of needed pages or can give the inquirer a view of needed pages by television.[46]

At the time of Dana's writing, television was in its earliest experimental stage. Seven years later, Paul Ott—a Belgian bibliographer and co-creator of the Universal Decimal Classification for books—said "Cinema, phonographs, radio, television: these instruments, taken as substitutes for the book, will in fact become the new book, the most powerful works for diffusion of human thought. This will be the radiated library, the televised book."[47] In 1939 Judson Jennings suggested that by 1976 television would make it possible "to read extracts in books that were thousands of miles away."[48] By 1948, the Library of Congress was able to give a public demonstration of Ultrafax, a technology "in which television and photography were combined to transmit information through the air at 186,000 miles a second."[49] In the demonstration, Ultrafax was used to transmit "the entire 1,047 pages of the novel *Gone With the Wind* across the city of Washington from the old Wardman-Park Hotel to a screen in the Library's Coolidge Auditorium in two minutes and twenty-one seconds."[50]

In 1951, an interlibrary teletype network was built following a catastrophe at the Michigan State Library:

> A disastrous fire had crippled the State Library, and teletype communications were used to link it with the Detroit Public Library, the University of Michigan Library, and the Grand Rapids Public Library in order to provide interim library services while the State Library rebuilt its own collection.[51]

Teletype promised "the speed of the telephone with the authority of the printed word"[52] and libraries eventually used it for remote reference services[53], interlibrary loan requests[54], business communications[55], and services for the deaf.[56]

In 1952, the inaugural issue of the journal *Library Trends* described itself as "a medium for evaluative recapitulation of current thought and practice, searching for those ideas and procedures which hold the greatest potentialities for the future."[57] This issue was a collection of thoughtful articles devoted to the theme of current trends in college and university libraries. Thirteen authors examined topics such as management, public relations, and buildings. One of the authors noted that "modern colleges and universities reflect the instability and changing character of the social order out of which they grow" and that "it is from these forces that library programs and practices evolve."[58] But the forces in the mind of Ellsworth were "the rapid growth of the university, the drastic adaptations made by universities during the last two World Wars, the vast extension of the scientific method, and the sudden development of the United States as a major world power."[59] Technology, as a force to reckon with in its own right, is absent from the discussion. Furthermore, the tenor of the articles reflects the luxury of a slower pace of change and the ability to reflect on change as it occurred. The future was important but not frantically urgent because it was not perceived as approaching at a blinding speed. The practice of responding to change read from present realities with gentle trend lines to the future had not been usurped by the regime of responding to change read from the future with disruptive disconnects from the present. Forecasting had not achieved the status of a driving factor in the decision-making process and technology was not seen as a driving factor in forecasting. The advent of digital computing would change all of this.

In 1955, there were less than twenty-five electronic computers in American universities.[60] It was, however, during the same decade that American libraries began the use of computers.[61] The National Library of Medicine began plans for what became MEDLARS[62] in 1957[63] and in hindsight, the project was a rubicon for the relationship between computers and libraries. This magnetic-tape based system was conceived as a tool that would perform many tasks, including journal indexing, patron search queries, interlibrary loans and inventory control.[64] When the MEDLARS project was completed in 1964, "there was no other publicly available fully operational electronic storage and retrieval system of its magnitude in existence."[65] At about the same time, the Massachusetts Institute of Technology was performing experiments with online information retrieval[66] but the early signals that computers would introduce a process of disruptive transformation were still at least a decade away. Indeed, as late as 1962 a report from the National Education Association suggested the use of the technology of vending machines in schools and colleges "for such things as automatic snack bars and automated libraries."[67]

In 1963, a report sponsored by the Council on Library Resources argued for computer automation at the Library of Congress because "with present methods, research libraries are failing to meet developing information needs … libraries should take advantage of modern technology in order to offer new, and hitherto unrealizable, services to their users."[68] This observation was echoed a year later by Alan Rees of the library science faculty at Western Reserve University: "The increasing complexity of modern civilization, the advent of the space age, and the consequent added significance of recorded knowledge have presented a serious challenge to the traditional practice of librarianship."[69] Florida Atlantic University opened in 1964 and the head of the library—given the title Director of the Library and Information Retrieval Services— "was hired with the stipulation that he would develop a computer-based library system."[70]

Examples of early computer applications in libraries include the American Library Association exhibition at the 1964 New York World's Fair, which showcased the "first public demonstration of an online bibliographic retrieval system;" in 1967, the Medical Research Library, Downstate Medical Center of the State University of New York, installed an online catalog for patron use; in 1968, the University of Chicago had an integrated library computer system with modules for acquisitions, serials control, and cataloging; in 1969, computer-based library circulation systems were in use; in 1970, the National Library of Medicine provided a "dial-up service for searching 100 key journals, available to a number of regional medical centres in the U.S.;" in 1972, the libraries of the constituent colleges of the California State University and Colleges system were able to exchange email.[71] During the 1970s, minicomputers were increasingly common and remote online services for shared cataloging, book purchasing, interlibrary loans and reference database searching proliferated.[72]

Print Media in Light of Alternative Information Formats

As communication technologies arose from the harnessing of electricity, their effects upon print communications began to draw the attention of forecasters. This naturally evolved into ideas about libraries and their main stock: print media.

During the late 19th century, "Octave Uzanne, an American writer and journalist, saw about him the portentous rise of a new communications technology."[73] In 1894, Uzanne published an article in *Scribner's Magazine Illustrated* titled "The End of Books,"[74] stating that due to "the progress of electricity and modern mechanism" the printing press was destined to "fall into desuetude as a means of current interpretation of our mental products" …printing was "threatened with death by the various devices for registering sound which have lately been invented, and which little by little will go on to perfection" and so "our grand-children will no longer trust their works to this somewhat antiquated process, now become very easy to replace by phonography, which is yet in its initial stage, and of which we have much to hope."[75] This migration from print to recorded sound would be a natural process because "reading …soon brings on great weariness; for not only does it require of the brain a sustained attention which consumes a large proportion of the cerebral phosphates, but it also forces our bodies into various fatiguing attitudes."[76] Uzanne concluded that "phonography will probably be the destruction of printing" and "libraries will be transformed into phonographotecks"[77] …"the printed book is about to disappear."[78]

Uzanne's nineteenth century forecast was one of the earliest "death of print" prognostications based on scenarios suggested by the power of modern communications technology. Furthermore, his assumptions and rationale foreshadowed analogous predictions that would populate the thinking of prominent thinkers throughout the twentieth century. Each new generation of technology was robed in scenarios ending in the death of print.

Along with Melville Dewey, Shiyali Ranganathan is considered one of the patriarchs of modern librarianship. In 1931, he wrote "who knows that a day may not come …when the dissemination of knowledge, which is the vital function of libraries, will be realized by libraries even by means other than those of the printed book?"[79] Beginning in the 1930s, microform was viewed as a promising alternative to the book. In 1936, historian Robert C. Binkley predicted that microfilm would "have and impact on the intellectual world comparable with that of the invention of printing."[80] Carl H. Milam of the American Library Association claimed in 1939 that

> among the new mechanical aids to learning, none are more certainly of great importance to libraries than those which make it possible to reproduce library

> materials photographically on film at small expense…
> the time will come when a good research library will
> undertake to supply its patrons on short notice with a
> copy of any book which exists in any library anywhere
> in the world.[81]

One year later, Harvard librarian Frederick Kilgour wrote that microfilm was "one of the most important developments in the trans-mission of the printed word since Gutenberg."[82] Fremont Rider of the Wesleyan University Library was so optimistic about micro-cards that he promoted the idea that storage costs associated with library growth could be reduced by "a full 100%."[83]

By 1963, a report from the Council on Library Resources to the Library of Congress projected that "progress in reproduction techniques, particularly from microfilm, has been so rapid that the circulation of most documents in their printed form may become unnecessary."[84] Numerous others during the 1960s described experimental advances in microform technology where such minute reductions had been achieved that the possibility placing the equivalent of millions of volumes on a single bookshelf of microform had become theoretically possible; further advances would enable the reduction of the holdings of the world's libraries to a few sheets.[85] Burnham Beckwith, an economist and statistician, proposed in 1967 that

> Since more and more new books and magazines will be
> published or reproduced on cheap microfilm slides…
> more and more readers will prefer to buy, read, and pre-
> serve such slides rather than books and magazines….
> By 2100, most new books will be produced on slides,
> which will then cost less than fifteen cents apiece."[86]

The ergonomics of microfiche readers was addressed in a 1968 ar-ticle in the *National Microform Association Journal*. What was needed was a "cuddly" reader, one that was as compact and comfortable as a book.[87]

Even into the 1970s microform was viewed by some as the most promising candidate for the transition to paperless journals.[88] As late as 1974, Yale sociologist Paul Starr believed that, due to microfiche, "it is quite likely that vast areas of publishing—academic research, technical literature, government reports, industrial publications, medical and educational records, even telephone books and commercial catalogs—may be largely taken out of the printed medium."[89] But the late 1960s also marked the beginning of the era of hope for a digital transformation of libraries.

Publishing "on demand" from digital files was described as a "likely trend" for the near future in 1963[90] and in 1965 Joseph Licklider, an MIT computer scientist who pioneered concepts that lead to the internet, was one of the first to call for a full substitution of computer-based information systems for libraries of print-on-paper:

> We need to substitute for the book a device that will make it easy to transmit information without transporting material, and that will not only present information to people but also processes it for them … a meld of library and computer is evidently required.[91]

University of California librarian William Webb predicted in 1977 that "in the year 2000 a large fraction (20-30 percent? 40-50 percent?) of what are now periodical articles will appear instead as abstracts available only on a CRT screen or on an individually ordered printout."[92] He further asserted that "I am certain that in the year 2000 the majority of academic libraries will give away microcopies of what we now call card catalogs. Every student and every faculty member will carry off what he or she wants."[93] Richard Roistacher of the University of Illinois Center for Advanced Computation described, in 1978, the future development of "virtual journals" delivered via computer networks,[94] and in 1979 Christopher Evans, who was considered—at that time—"one of the world's leading authorities on microprocessors"[95] explained that due to computer technology "the 1980s will see the book … begin a steady slide into oblivion."[96]

During the 1970s and 1980s, Wilfred Lancaster of the graduate school of library science at the University of Illinois at Urbana-Champaign became somewhat of an icon in library forecasting circles. In 1978, he suggested that "the 'librarian' of the year 2000 may be a freelance information specialist, working from the office or from the home… In this environment, 'consulting the librarian' would mean using a terminal to contact an information specialist."[97] The following year he coauthored an imaginary history written from the perspective of the year 2001. According to this history, the last paper encyclopedia was published in 1993, print on paper virtually disappeared for "much of the primary literature of the sciences and the social science" by 1995, and by 2001 textbooks had been "virtually eliminated" and print on paper was "the exception rather than the rule."[98] In 1982 he helped produce an extensive Delphi study on the impact of a paperless society on the research library of the future[99], and in the same year he published a book titled *Libraries and Librarians in an Age of Electronics.*[100] There Lancaster asserted that "the next few years will see a rapid and inevitable move away from print on paper toward paperless communication. It is my belief that the paperless system could materialize by the year 2000" and that by the year 2000 "libraries as we now know them will become obsolete."[101]

During the mid-1980s, Columbia University librarian Patricia Battin attenuated the somewhat monolithic views of Lancaster. She did speak of the "advent of the wired scholar" and "the end of the printed page as the sole means of scholarly communication and information storage and retrieval."[102] Battin did not, however, foresee a purely paperless system, warning that it would be a mistake to move forward by building systems "from the imperative of the technological capacities rather than from the perspective and requirements of the scholar and student."[103] In a radical suggestion for the time, Battin proposed that "the obvious answer to the Electronic Scholar's plight is the formation of a Scholarly Information Center by merging the Libraries and Computer Center to provide an information infra-structure to stimulate the continuous autonomous use of information sources."[104]

In 1981 Thomas Hickey, a researcher at OCLC, wrote that due to technology, "in the long term, the library can be expected to concentrate primarily on unique materials and to move closer to our current idea of an archive"[105] and that "the paper journals of today will soon be supplanted by journals available primarily over electronic networks."[106] As a consequence, Hickey predicted that "huge capital investments will not be needed to maintain access to the journal literature from the early 1980s onward. All that will be needed is an investment in fairly standard office equipment and a scheme for access to the databases."[107] Susan Crooks wrote in a 1982 Library of Congress publication that "there is every reason for very serious concern for the survival of libraries" but added that "there is also reason for believing that vital roles for libraries will continue," cautioning that "futurist stances must simplify the complex factors influencing the course of development in order to evoke usefully vivid images."[108]

In the late 1970s, libraries began to explore the possibilities of laser videodisc technology.[109] The theme of the 1979 Frankfurt Book Fair was "The Videodisc: Challenge and Opportunity for Publishers"[110] *New York* magazine published a home electronics special issue in November of 1980. The cover image featured a videodisc with the phrase "Here Comes the Videodisc." The feature article included comments from MIT technology visionary Nicholas Negroponte. According to Negroponte, the videodisc had "nothing to do with movies … that's not what it's about;" instead, "it is a book, a surrogate book."[111] The following year, IBM vice president Lewis M. Branscomb agreed: "the really attractive storage medium for books" was "not paper or magnetic material, but the optical videodisc."[112] He noted that "something approaching the text content of 3,200 books could be contained on a single, two-sided disc" and that "once a master disc is prepared, thousands of discs can be replicated and sold for less than the cost of a single book today."[113]

In a 1985 article—"Good bye Gutenberg"—published by *PC Magazine* we were given the news that due to primarily economic factors, "we can easily say that in the year 2000 electronic publishing will be the only reasonable way to present all the material we have."[114] Yale anthropologist Timothy Weiskel, writing for *College and Research Libraries* in 1986, agreed: "libraries, as we have come to know them, are an endangered species, and they may well become extinct."[115] In his view, the book is a "piece of late medieval technology" and new computer based technologies offered "more efficient, less costly, and more convenient channels for information."[116]

CD ROM databases were introduced in 1985[117] and during the latter half of the 1980s, this was the reigning new technology. Silver Platter Information Services introduced the ERIC database on CD ROM,[118] Grolier began selling *Academic American Encyclopedia* in the new format,[119] and CD ROM librarianship emerged with its own journal: *CD-ROM Librarian*.[120]

In 1986, Microsoft published a (paper) book about CD ROM titled *The New Papyrus* in which Bill Gates encouraged readers to see CD ROM as the "summation" of "television, movies, video, slides, audio, [and] books."[121] Jerry Pournelle of *InfoWorld Magazine* said "CD ROM will change the world"[122] and an article in *Library Hi Tech* described the medium as a "revolution in the making."[123] In 1989 *The Times of London* described a CD ROM based electronic book—the Dynabook—and concluded that "The concept of the electronic book, once predicted eventually to replace the printed version entirely, is becoming increasingly technically feasible."[124] Sony produced a CD based electronic book in 1991, the Data Discman,[125] but after peaking around 1997 CD ROM based content publishing "dwindled to near-insignificance."[126]

In 1988, sociologist David Lyon observed that

> Little doubt exists among many popular commentators that the advanced nations are entering a new phase: the information society. Forecasts abound of the massive social impacts of new information technologies of computing and telecommunications. Time-honoured social institutions and lifestyles are said to be undergoing transformation.[127]

The library, as one of those time-honored social institutions, would not escape transformation. The 1989 annual report from the Council on Library Resources spoke of "new demands implicit in a technology-driven future" and concluded that "what a library is and needs to be has changed for all time."[128] Former library school dean Anne Woodsworth wrote the same year that "information technology, which is continuing to develop at an exponential rate, will provide universities and libraries with unforeseeable opportunities for the creation, storage, and transmission of information."[129] On the popular front, *Money* magazine announced that "electronic books will organize your life, replace your library, and fit in your pocket."[130]

The next few years were especially heady times as the Internet became a part of the public consciousness. In 1990, a book on the future of the research library observed that computer-based technologies "are altering, before our eyes, what we are doing and have been doing for years, decades, even centuries."[131] By 1992, John Kountz—a library automation director at California State University—declared that

> If a library means books, then being a librarian… may be an endangered career. In the next five years or so,

the market for—and the availability of—information printed on paper can be anticipated to shrink by 50 percent. By the turn of the century, paper will satisfy less than 5 percent of the total commerce in information.[132]

At the same time the university librarian at the University of Minnesota, Eldred Smith, wrote optimistically about our liberation from "the print prison" and how e-mail "offers the advantages of print with few of print's shortcomings."[133] One year later, World Bank librarian Sylvia Piggott echoed Kountz: "We will not be far into the 21st century before the librarian's role in the information retrieval process disappears in the face of perfected end user access."[134]

Between 1991 and 1993, Ray Kurzweil—an MIT trained expert in artificial intelligence—wrote a series of nineteen futuristic articles for *Library Journal.* During that period, he envisioned that by the early 2000s

electronic books will have enormous advantages, with pictures that can move and interact with the user, increasingly intelligent search paradigms, simulated environments that the user can enter and explore, and vast quantities of accessible material. Yet vital to its ability to truly make the paper book obsolete is that the essential qualities of paper and ink will have been fully matched. The book will enter obsolescence.[135]

Kurzweil went on to declare that "with books in virtual form, transmitted readily through the communications ether, the emerging virtual library will not need to be housed in a building."[136] Lauren H. Seiler and Thomas T. Surprenant—a sociologist of technology and a librarian—declared in 1993 that "the end of the print library is in sight"[137] and Jordan Scepanski of the Triangle Research Libraries Network in North Carolina speculated in 1995 that "the position of today's library director might evolve in a number of different ways, or perhaps might disappear. The director could be a warehouse coordinator, a study hall administrator, or a manager of technicians."[138] At the same time, MIT faculty member Nicholas Negroponte claimed that "the slow human handling of most information in the form of books, magazines, and videocassettes, is about to become the instantaneous and inexpensive transfer of electronic data that move at the speed of light."[139] During the mid-1990s, as the rate of visionary notions of what the Internet would bring increased, Rider University librarian John Buschman cautioned that "it is questionable whether as a profession we have given any real reflective thought or inquiry to the public consequences to print literacy, the historical record, and social memory."[140]

In 1995—the same year that the first free Web browser became publicly available[141]—Virginia Tech University bibliographer Paul Metz offered a contrarian note:

> In time, nearly everything will be available in electronic form, but it doesn't follow that it will be used that way. Whoever asked why you would want to read The Miller's Tale on a computer screen asked a good question. Yet having Chaucer in electronic form will be very valuable for people who want to find a passage or count word frequencies or trace the use of a concept. There's a wonderful sequence in the film Slow Fires in which Daniel Boorstin reminds us of the predictions that radio would doom the telephone and TV would doom radio and points out that, of course, both the telephone and the radio are doing better than they were when their supposed successors were invented. So a mixed mode is possible for a long time.[142]

In contrast to the all-digital vision, the theme of a long term mixed mode was expressed by several others in the same general time period. Roger Fidler wrote in 1998 that "paper has many redeeming qualities that will be difficult, if not impossible, for digital systems to entirely replace."[143] At the time, Fidler was the director of the Cyber Media Research Center at Kent State University and the journal that published his article—*Future of Print Media Journal*—was an "online only" publication sponsored by Kent State. The journal no longer exists and back issues are not available. Nevertheless, in 1999, the vice president of technology development at Microsoft predicted that "twenty years from now paper will be a thing of the past."[144] Rounding out the twentieth century, Walt Crawford of the Research Libraries Group observed that "no given future is inevitable, but a complex future of analog and digital media seems both most likely and most desirable for most libraries and users."[145]

In 2000, Larry Hardesty, then president of the Association of College and Research Libraries made a practical observation rarely taken into account in the all-digital proposals of the day:

> Relatively few of the millions of journals and books that fill our academic libraries have been retrospectively converted to digital formats and there is no evidence that a significant percentage will be in the foreseeable future. In addition, there has been little evidence of any abatement in the current publication rate of print materials, and most remain unavailable digitally.[146]

John Buschman offered this caution the same year: "When we convert print to electronic formats heedlessly, without planning for, paying for, or worrying about preservation of these new artifacts, we are evacuating the historical record for the future."[147] Recent book scanning projects by Google and others notwithstanding, Hardesty and Buschman's comments remain an overlooked but crucial point of practical concern.

The following year Bradley Schaffner, Slavic Studies Librarian at the University of Kansas, asserted that "the belief of many people that electronic formats are superior to other formats is too simplistic."[148] Schaffner warned that a massive investment in digital information formats creates an artificial need to justify the expenses in terms of the purported superiority of digital formats. But the commonly assumed superiority is not intrinsic: "One should not consider electronic resources superior to other formats simply because they use current technology. Library resources need to be evaluated and acquired based not on format but, instead, on content and patron and disciplinary need."[149] In the same vein, Suzanne Thorin, speaking in 2001 as dean of the university libraries at Indiana University, maintained that "despite their growth, electronic resources will never replace the knowledge already captured in books for centuries."[150]

These examples of cautionary thoughts on the all-digital vision are not, however, representative of the weightiest portion of the literature.[151]

More indicative of the dominant zeitgeist is a statement from an e-book publisher in 2000 that the children of today's undergraduates "are maybe never going to see a book."[152] The undergraduates of 2000 now have children and children's books are still being published. Nevertheless, in 2002 a statement from the National Research Council anticipated that "the distinction between the book and the library may itself become blurred as the Internet evolves into a seamless mesh for probing the world's 'collection.'"[153] The vice president for information technologies at Cornell University, Polley McClure, and Columbia University librarian James Neal wrote in 2003 that they expected a "massive conversion of print to electronic resources in library collections."[154] Shortly thereafter, forecasts were full of exciting visions sparked by the Google Print project. In 2004 *The New York Times* declared that "it may redefine the nature of the university"[155] and *USA Today* announced that "this is the day the world changes."[156]

Conclusion

As noted earlier: Initial adoption patterns, long term diffusion, and the bearing these have on the lasting significance of a new technology are phenomena that can be described in hindsight but not predicted or controlled through foresight. But Alex Wright, author of *Glut: Mastering Information Through the Ages,* has observed that hindsight and technology are not natural companions: "the computer creates a teleology of progress" that "works against historical perception."[157] Consider the lead phrase of a recent ad from Intel: "Today is so yesterday."[158] Classics professor Stephen Bertman believes that "the shorter our cultural memory, the more uncritical our acceptance of what we are shown. By denying our eyes the lens of history, we validate the correctness of our myopia."[159] Persuasive forecasts have the power to shape decision making related to the deployment of large amounts of human, capital, and physical resources. But when forecasts are not tempered by the lens of history—if our "prime and unchallenged directive is to keep up with change"[160]—we run the risk of inducing costly forgetfulness and a hackneyed repetitiveness. Notwithstanding the teleology of progress, the intellectual discipline of "looking squarely backward"[161] may be the true high ground.

Still the literature suggests that the pace of cultural change continues to increase, the stakes for libraries remain high, and the perceived need to anticipate the future is undiminished. This is illustrated by the countless thousands of forecasts that have been offered for libraries in recent decades. Whereas libraries have been progressive implementers of technology for centuries, the development of new communications technologies has produced a steady flow of forecasts related to how these technologies could affect—even replace—libraries. Differing opinions abound, but all share the view that the effects are far from neutral.

And so the future continues to beckon and decision makers are compelled to envision the path ahead. Library related professional literature dedicated to technology forecasts continues to flow. Note the current bustle around the concept of "Library 2.0" and even "Beyond Library 2.0." Books with titles like *Library 2.0 and Beyond: Innovative Technologies and Tomorrow's User*[162] and articles titled "Journey to Library 2.0"[163] and "Surfing the Library 2.0 Wave"[164] and "Library 2.0: The New E-World Order"[165] populate the latest additions to library catalogs and periodical databases. The power of a forecast, by whatever name, to influence thoughts about the future and to affect decision making in the present *remains* a topic worthy of reflection. But contrary to the economist Burnham Beckwith—who claimed in 1967 that scientifically precise prediction was possible for up to five hundred years into the future[166]—the astronomer Erich Jantsch was more prescient when he said, also in 1967, that "technological forecasting is not yet a science but an art, and is characterized today by attitudes, not tools."[167]

So, libraries and technology have a long history of symbiosis. The uniform *pattern* of this symbiosis, however, is a maze of starts, stops, unanticipated forks and amazing discoveries. Achievement of the amazing discoveries is perhaps never a straightforward or clear-cut process. This is crucially important to keep in mind when technology is part of large scale, high consequence decision making. For, as the next chapter argues, standard decision making models fail to account for the sometimes heartbreaking reality that high consequence decision making is—like technological progress—never a straightforward or clear-cut process.

Notes

1. Wheelwright, *Heraclitus*, 29.
2. Cicero, *De Divinatione*, 223.
3. Tocqueville, *Democracy in America*, 259–260.

4. Karabell, *A Visionary Nation: Four Centuries of American Dreams and What Lies Ahead*, 4.

5. Clarke, "All Our Yesterdays," 251.

6. Sherden, *The Fortune Sellers: The Big Business of Buying and Selling Predictions*, 5.

7. Wheelwright and Makridakis, *Forecasting Methods for Management*, 1.

8. Rogers, *Diffusion of Innovations*, 4th ed., 8.

9. Ibid., 16, italics added.

10. Ibid., 31.

11. Sapp and Gilmour, "A Brief History of Academic Libraries," 553–554.

12. Query syntax: (SU library* and (techno* or digit* or online or virtual or web or internet or computer*) and (forecast* or trend* or futur* or predict)) performed March 31, 2009.

13. In the 1950s only one item appears; in the 1960s: 183; in the 1970s: 732; in the 1980s: 1,667; in the 1990s: 3,718; since 2000: 5,983. The volume of articles related to academic libraries is roughly twice that of articles related to public libraries.

14. Query syntax: (SU library* and (techno* or digit* or online or virtual or web or internet or computer*) and (forecast* or trend* or futur* or predict)) performed April 8, 2009.

15. Stevens, "A Popular History of Library Technology."

16. Winsor, "Telephones in Libraries."

17. Garnett, "Electric Light at the British Museum Reading Room."

18. Soule, *How to Plan a Library Building for Library Work*, 202.

19. Headicar, *The Library of the Future*, 76.

20. Brown, "Cataloguing Appliances."

21. Kroeger, "Instruction in Cataloging in Library Schools," 111.

22. Schwab, "The Use of the Teleautograph at Yale University."

23. Drury, "Labor-savers in Library Service," 538.

24. Soule, *How to Plan a Library Building for Library Work*, 217.

25. Anonymous, "Discussion on duplicating processes."

26. Swingle, "Utilization of Photographic Methods in Library Research Work."

27. Anonymous, "Fine Computer: A New Mechanical Device."

28. Becker, "The Future of Library Automation and Information Networks," 4.

29. Arms, "The Technological Context," 14.

30. Plummer, "Photograph Collection of Pratt Institute Free Library," 637.

31. Fairchild, "Lantern Slides for Lectures in Library Work With Children," 156.

32. Babcock, "Special Material in Libraries," 155–156.

33. Anonymous, "Moving Pictures in Library Work."

34. Wright, "Use of the Victrola in the Story Hour," 126.

35. Anonymous, "Player Piano Roles," 95.

36. Anonymous, "Gramaphones in the Public Library as an Aid to Teaching Foreign Languages," 277–278.

37. Anonymous, "Phonograph Record Collection at St. Paul (Minn.) Library," 133.

38. Anonymous, *The Woman's College Library: The Present and the Future*, 11.

39. Milam, "Experimentation," 50.

40. Shera, "Tomorrow, and Tomorrow, and Tomorrow!," 278.

41. Iles, "The Work of Traveling Libraries," 30.

42. Dewey, *Traveling Libraries*, 7–8.
43. Headicar, *The Library of the Future*, 38.
44. Dana, *Changes in Library Methods in a Changing World.*
45. Ibid., 3.
46. Ibid., 10.
47. Ott quoted in Wright, *Glut: Mastering Information Through the Ages*, 185.
48. Jennings, "Extension of Library Service," 79.
49. Rohrbach, *FIND: Automation at the Library of Congress, the First Twenty-five Years and Beyond*, 7.
50. Ibid.
51. Becker, "The Future of Library Automation," 4–5.
52. Advertisement for Telex, *The Economist 179 (1956):* 867.
53. Olson et al. "Statewide Teletype Reference Service," 203–209.
54. Morris, "Experiences With a Library Network," 39–44.
55. Poole, "Teletypewriters in Libraries: a State of the Art Report," 283–286.
56. Store and Way, "Teletypewriter Service for the Deaf," 4.
57. Anonymous, [Masthead].
58. Ellsworth, "Trends in Higher Education Affecting the College and University Library," 17–18.
59. Ibid., 18.
60. Perlis, "The Computer in the University," 181.
61. Adams, *Information Technology & Libraries: A Future for Academic Libraries*, 1.
62. Medical Literature Analysis and Retrieval System
63. Rogers, "The Development of MEDLARS," 150–151.
64. Wyndham, *A History of the National Library of Medicine: The Nation's Treasury of Medical Knowledge*, 370.
65. Ibid., 374–375.
66. Thompson, *The End of Libraries*, 34.
67. Finn, et al., *Automation in Educational Administration: Vending Machines in Schools and Colleges.*
68. Council on Library Resources, *Automation and the Library of Congress*, v.
69. Rees, "Librarians and Information Centers," 200.
70. Heiliger, "Florida Atlantic University: New Libraries on New Campuses," 181.
71. Adams, *Information Technology & Libraries*, 1–9 and Becker, *"The Future of Library Automation,"* 4.
72. Arms, "The Technological Context," 19.
73. Frank A. Biocca, "The pursuit of sound: radio, perception and utopia in the early twentieth century," 61.
74. Uzanne, "The End of Books."
75. Ibid., 224.
76. Ibid.
77. Ibid., 224–225.
78. Ibid., 230.
79. Shiyali Ranganathan, *The Five Laws of Library Science*, 414.
80. Binkley quoted in Cady, "The Electronic Revolution in Libraries: Microfilm Déjà vu?," 375.

81. Milam, "Experimentation," 51.
82. Kilgour quoted in Cady, "The Electronic Revolution in Libraries," 375.
83. Rider, *The Scholar and the Future of the Research Library: A Problem and Its Solution*, 101.
84. Council on Library Resources, *Automation and the Library of Congress*, 10.
85. Kaser, "Automation in Libraries of the Future." | Platt, "Where Will the Books Go?" | Leimkuhler and Neville, "The Uncertain Future of the Library."
86. Beckwith, *The Next 500 Years: Scientific Predictions of Major Social Trends*, 202.
87. Wooster, "Towards a Uniform Federal Report Numbering System and a Cuddly Microfiche Reader," 63–69.
88. Sondak and Schwartz, "The Paperless Journal," 82–83.
89. Starr, "Transforming the Libraries: From Paper to Microfiche," 35.
90. Council on Library Resources, *Automation and the Library of Congress*, 10.
91. Licklider, *Libraries of the Future*, 6.
92. Webb, "Collection Development for the University and Large Research Library," 141.
93. Ibid., 143.
94. Roistacher, "The Virtual Journal," 18–24.
95. Evans, *The Micro Millennium*, ii.
96. Ibid., 115.
97. Lancaster, *Toward Paperless Information Systems*, 158.
98. Lancaster, Drasgow, and Marks, "The Changing Face of the Library: A Look at Libraries and Librarians in the Year 2001," 55–77.
99. Lancaster, Drasgow, and Marks, *The Impact of a Paperless Society on the Research Library of the Future.*
100. Lancaster, *Libraries and Librarians in an Age of Electronics.*
101. Ibid., 87, 151.
102. Battin, "The Electronic Library—A Vision for the Future," 12.
103. Ibid., 13.
104. Ibid., 16. | This theme continued to attract attention as late as 2000, as represented in Larry Hardesty ed., *Books, Bytes, and Bridges.*
105. Hickey, "The Journal in the Year 2000," 256.
106. Ibid., 260.
107. Ibid.
108. Crooks, "Libraries in the Year 2000," 1.
109. Mehnert, "National Library of Medicine," 74.
110. Lottman, "Frankfurt Book Fair, 1979," 488.
111. Schrage, "Good-bye, 'Dallas,' Hello, Videodiscs," 38.
112. Branscomb, "The Electronic Library," 148.
113. Ibid., 149.
114. Jeffries, "Good bye Gutenberg!," 96.
115. Weiskel, "Libraries as Life-systems: Information, Entropy, and Coevolution on Campus," 545.
116. Ibid., 561.
117. Tenopir, "What's Happening with CD-ROM," 50–51.
118. Miller, "Silver Platter: Dishing Up Data for Libraries," 23–39.

119. Slutsker and Par, "Waiting for New Hardware," 262.

120. Publication commenced in 1987 and ceased in 1992.

121. Lambert and Ropiequet, eds., *The New Papyrus: The Current and Future State of the Art*, xi.

122. Ibid., back cover quote.

123. Helgerson, "CD-ROM: A Revolution in the Making."

124. May, "The Book Opens a New Chapter; Electronic book."

125. Rogers, "Sony's Electronic Book: A New Library Format?," 26.

126. Crawford, "Where Have All the CD-ROMs Gone?," 66–68.

127. Lyon, *The Information Society: Issues and Illusions*, vii.

128. Council on Library Resources, *33rd Annual Report: 1989, 25.*

129. Woodsworth, "The Model Research Library: Planning for the Future," 136.

130. Hedberg, "Electronic Books Will Organize your Life, Replace Your Library and Fit In Your Pocket," 183.

131. Smith, *The Librarian, the Scholar, and the Future of the Research Library*, 1.

132. Kountz, "Tomorrow's Libraries: More Than a Modular Telephone Jack, Less Than a Complete Revolution," 39.

133. Smith, "The Print Prison," 50.

134. Piggott, "The Virtual Library: Almost There," 206.

135. Kurzweil, "The Future of Libraries Part 2: The End of Books," 141.

136. Kurzweil, "The Virtual Library," 55.

137. Seiler and Surprenant, "The Virtual Information Center: Scholars and Information in the Twenty-first Century," 157.

138. Scepanski, "Forecasting, Forestalling, Fashioning: The Future of Academic Libraries and Librarians," 173.

139. Negroponte, *Being Digital*, 4.

140. Buschman, "Librarians, Self-censorship, and Information Technologies," 223.

141. Anonymous, "Mosaic Network Navigator Offered Free on the Internet," 67.

142. Metz, "The View From a University Library," 33.

143. Fidler, "Life After 2001: Redefining Print Media in the Cyber Age."

144. Kahney, "Microsoft: Paper Is Dead."

145. Crawford, *Being Analog: Creating Tomorrow's Libraries*, 28.

146. Hardesty, "Do We Need Academic Libraries?"

147. Buschman, "On Libraries and the Public Sphere," 5.

148. Schaffner, "Electronic Resources: A Wolf in Sheep's Clothing?," 248.

149. Ibid.

150. Thorin, "Why Libraries?," ¶ 7.

151. This is true for every era. Suggestions that the promises of the all-digital environment might need more careful scrutiny are *far* less common than forecasts predicated on the belief that the superiority of an all-digital environment is beyond scrutiny.

152. Moldow, "Publish or Perish," 72.

153. National Research Council, *Preparing for the Revolution: Information Technology and the Future of the Research University*, 33.

154. Neal and McClure, "Organizing Information Resources for Effective Management," 42–43.

155. *New York Times*, "The Electronic Library," A28.
156. *USA Today*, "Google to Scan Books From Big Libraries," ¶ 9.
157. Wright, *Glut: Mastering Information Through the Ages*, 3.
158. This was an ephemeral ad on the *New York Times* website, *May 11, 2009.*
159. Bertman, *Hyperculture: The Cost of Human Speed*, 27.
160. Ibid., 1.
161. Wright, *Glut: Mastering Information Through the Ages*, 3.
162. Courtney, ed., *Library 2.0 and Beyond: Innovative Technologies and Tomorrow's User.*
163. Hastings, "Journey to Library 2.0."
164. Huwe, "Surfing the Library 2.0 Wave."
165. Pin, "Library 2.0: The New E-World Order."
166. Beckwith, *The Next 500 Years: Scientific Predictions of Major Social Trends,* ix, x.
167. Jantsch, *Technological Forecasting in Perspective*, 17.

CHAPTER TWO

Institutional Decision Making: Not Just Politics

Institutional decision making is rarely, if ever, a straightforward transaction. An oversimplified interpretation of the process can prevent the kind of insight needed for fruitful progress. This is especially true in high consequence decision situations such as building programs and large scale technology purchasing.

Introduction

As seen in chapter one, technology rarely—if ever—yields the amazing results we crave without taking us through a maze of starts, stops, and unanticipated forks. In this chapter we will see that standard decision making models do not adequately account for the fact that large scale institutional decision making takes us through the same maze. When technology is in the mix, the effects can be daunting.

The literature on decision making is immense. Fifty years ago, William Gore and Fred Silander, wrote "A Bibliographical Essay on Decision Making" for *Administrative Science Quarterly*. They stated that "there is a large body of literature dealing more or less with some facet of decision making. A generous list might run to five thousand entries."[1] Today that list has multiplied twenty-five times.[2]

The staggering number of publications on decision making is spread across many disciplines. As noted by John Payne of Duke University, "the study of organizational decision making is intensely interdisciplinary, employing concepts, models, and methods from anthropology, economics, political science, psychology, sociology, statistics, and other fields."[3] Furthermore, decision making is an unusually complex process:

> As an activity, it takes place at various levels—individual, collective, group, and organizational—and it

involves such diverse variables as the cognitive capabilities of the decision maker's mind, the communication of ideas and values among individuals, and the mathematical calculations that are intended to identify the optimal choice.[4]

Despite the immensity and complexity of the literature, however, scholars generally agree that models relevant to decision making in the higher education setting are relatively few in number.

In 1971 John Baldridge wrote a book, *Power and Conflict in the University: Research in the Sociology of Complex Organizations,* in which he noted that "the study of universities as organizations has typically relied on one of two organizational paradigms."[5] These he identified as the bureaucratic and the collegial. But, finding these lacking, Baldridge proposed a third model, the political.

At nearly the same time—in 1972—Michael Cohen, James March, and Johan Olsen published their now legendary article on the garbage can model.[6] Ellen Chaffee, writing for National Center for Higher Education Management Systems in 1983, included one more model—the rational—observing that "research that describes decision making at colleges and universities argues that the process…falls into [five categories]."[7] According to Chaffee, those categories, representing "certain patterns of assumptions and behaviors that seem to appear together… have become widely known as organizational decision models: collegial, bureaucratic, political, anarchical, and rational."[8] Chaffee's anarchical model is the same as the garbage can model described by Cohen, March, and Olsen. Though some scholars offer descriptions of decision making models based on a different rubric or variant taxonomy[9], these tend to be either subsets or reformulations of features found in the five models identified by Chaffee, or novel proposals not yet represented by an accumulated body of research. An overview of each of Chaffee's five decision making models is provided in the sections below.

The Rational Decision Making Model

In his book *The Psychology of Judgment and Decision Making,* Scott Plous observes that "early models of decision making assumed that people had a fixed set of attitudes and preferences that did not change as a function of how they were elicited. Decision makers were treated as 'rational actors.'"[10] The motto of this model might be "The rational executive bases his decision on the weight of evidence."[11] Building on this premise, rational decision making models "assume a very high capacity of the actors to collect information, to process it, and to draw proper conclusions from the information and its interpretation."[12] For instance a work from the 1960s asserted that the rational manager must

> …know what information he has about any problem, what information he doesn't have and how he can get it, and how he can use all the information he has to the best advantage in getting the problem solved. He must be as perceptive in recognizing, before the fact, what information will be relevant and important and what will not as he is in recognizing, with the benefit of hindsight, the obvious relevance and importance of certain information.[13]

Additional assumptions of the rational decision making model include "an economic, quantifiable, maximizing objective"…"stability of preferences over time"…"unlimited information processing"…"the existence of well-defined mutually exclusive alternatives"…"perfect estimates of outcomes and calculations of the expected value of each alternative"…decision makers who "are fully aware of the benefits arising from a decision and choose the alternative or outcome which provides the maximum benefit" and unlimited time and inexpensive information.[14]

But as early as the 1960s Herbert Simon of Carnegie-Melon University cautioned that "fascination with the pure theory of rational choice has sometimes distracted attention from the problems of decision makers who possess modest calculating powers in the face of a world of enormous complexity."[15] This asymmetry between calculating power and complexity leads to a quandary where "in the presence of uncertainty, people are often reluctant to think through the implications of each outcome."[16] Other researchers have concluded that "the theory of rational choice fails as a description of actual behavior,"[17] that rational models "provide little guidance as to how decisions are actually made at complex universities or about how individual colleges behave,"[18] and that "empirical objections to rational choice are so voluminous that they are, in effect, a laundry list of problems."[19]

Whereas "the concept of rational action starts from the idea that individuals should not make systematic mistakes,"[20] scholarly studies on rational choice have not produced a coherent body of evidence in support of the rational model.[21] Instead, research indicates that "choice behavior is not solely based on logical reasoning but is also influenced by biases, schemata, framing, and cognitive and judgmental heuristics."[22] Additional influences include "selective perception, pressures toward cognitive consistency, biases in memory, and changes in context."[23] Intractable limitations of the human condition curtail pure rationality:

> Decision makers use only part of the information that potentially is available, both because they are cognitively limited and can handle only so much information at a time, and because there are resource constraints on acquiring complete information even if it is available. Decisions often are made when a sufficient option is encountered (called "sufficing") rather than after a prolonged search for the best option.[24]

Finally, experimental studies indicate that there exists a point after which ever more information, a hallmark of the rational decision making model, has the bewildering effect of reducing accuracy while increasing confidence.[25] Despite scholarly efforts to rehabilitate the rational model,[26] it fails as a descriptive tool for gaining insight into decision making in higher education.[27]

The Political Decision Making Model

The 1971 work of Victor Baldridge, *Power and Conflict in the University: Research in the Sociology of Complex Organizations*, is considered a benchmark in the study of political decision making in higher education. Baldridge, then on the faculty at Stanford, outlined a political model centering on the notions of interest groups, power, and conflict. Interest groups with varying types and levels of power engage in conflict in order to influence decision outcomes. The question at the center of the political process is "How does a powerful group exert its pressure, what threats or promises can it make, and how does it translate its desires into political capital?"[28]

In this model, power is a commodity that can be possessed, accrued, and deployed. Stanford professor Jeffrey Pfeffer believes that

It is critical to be able to diagnose the power of other
players, including potential allies and possible oppo-
nents. We need to know who we are up against. Know-
ing where power comes from also helps us to build our
own power and thereby increase our capacity to take
action....we also need to know how to develop sources
of power and how to employ that power strategically
and tactically.[29]

The challenge, according to this model, is to understand the sources
of power, how to accrue it, how to assess the power of others, and how
to use power to prevail in the accomplishment of one's preferences.

In the view of some, the use of power in decision making is essential
because "mechanisms are required to resolve differences in preferences
and beliefs about what actions will produce what outcomes. Even the
most objective indicators are open to different interpretation;" so because
"organizational participants derive different meanings from the same
set of details" power must be used to resolve the impasse.[30]

But though "politics" is a common explanation for how things
"really" get done, the practical use of power metrics as a descriptive
construct is an extremely complex challenge for anyone attempting to
apply or test this framework in real institutional settings. In the end,
"despite superior resources and sanctioning power, organizational elites
are often unable to maximize their preferences."[31] This is because

[P]articipation, multiple bases of power, and interaction dynamics affect power relationships. Linkages
between decision processes and power, and between
power and organizational consequences, are mediated
by characteristics of the organizational environment,
decision tasks, and individual motives.[32]

Furthermore, as noted by James March of Stanford, power is
domain specific:

A person powerful in one domain is not necessarily
powerful in another. There is not a single index of
power for an individual decision maker, but differ-

ent powers for different decision arenas. The domain specificity of power is observed not only in government but also in business firms, families, and churches.[33]

Hence, the distribution of power and how it manifests is neither static, nor quantifiable, nor predictable. Decision making viewed through the political model can describe the past in terms of *subsets* of decision making phenomena related to power, but a normative transferable construct is more difficult to distill.

The Bureaucratic Decision Making Model

The fountainhead of scholarly thought on bureaucratic decision making is found in the writings of the great sociologist Max Weber.[34] Weber's commitment to this model is unambiguous:

> Experience tends universally to show that the purely bureaucratic type of administrative organization—that is, the monocratic variety of bureaucracy—is, from a purely technical point of view, capable of attaining the highest degree of efficiency and is in this sense formally the most rational known means of carrying out imperative control over human beings. It is superior to any other form in precision, in stability, in the stringency of its discipline, and in its reliability. It thus makes possible a particularly high degree of calculability of results for the heads of the organization and for those acting in relation to it. It is finally superior both in intensive efficiency and in the scope of its operations, and is formally capable of application to all kinds of administrative tasks.[35]

According to Weber, there are four essential characteristics of bureaucracy: the presence of jurisdictional areas arranged by administrative regulations, a fixed distribution of official duties, strictly delimited command authority, and a methodical provision for continuous fulfillment of officially designated functions.[36] The bureaucratic decision making model "portrays a setting where organizational decisions are consequences of the programs and programming of the units involved."[37]

Yet close observations of bureaucratic decision making structures reveal that this approach is prone to endemic dysfunctions such as "rigidity and inflexibility" and the tendency for rules "intended to assure uniformity of action throughout the organization [to] represent a statement of the least acceptable level of employee behavior."[38] In addition, scholars have noted that the bureaucratic model as a conceptual framework pays inadequate attention to "cognitive factors in decision making,"[39] "the interplay of individual attitudes, motives, goals,"[40] and "the different modes and styles of leadership that prevail."[41]

Consequently,

> the bureaucratic model tells us much about authority—that is, legitimate, formalized power—but not much about informal types of power and influence… it explains much about the organization's formal structure but little about the dynamic processes that characterize the organization in action…it also ignores political issues such as the struggles of various interest groups within the university.[42]

Finally, in a university setting, "each of the subsystems operates according to its own particular logic. This leads to fundamental paradoxes that underlie even the most inherent processes in universities."[43]

The Collegial Decision Making Model

Collegial decision making occurs in a setting where "significant decisions are taken in common by a small, face-to-face body with no single member dominating their initiation or determination [and] with all its members enjoying equal legal status and powers."[44] A variation of this pure form of collegiality "may also exist informally, however, in institutions in which one individual enjoys formal supremacy."[45] The primary emphases of collegial decision making are "participation, consensus, professional expertise and competency."[46]

The collegial model has been critiqued, however, as "more of a revolutionary ideology and a utopian projection than a description of the real shape of governance at any university."[47] So, though "there is nobility in the notion of people pooling their wisdom and muzzling their egos to make decisions that are acceptable—and fair—to all"[48] the reality is that "those who have examined collegial leadership have been inclined to stress its limitations, or, indeed, its obsolescence as a mode of governance in complex modern societies."[49]

Two impediments to the realization of collegial ideals are the size and diversity of college campuses and the psychological dynamics of groups convened for collegial decision making tasks: "size and increasing professionalization have left only vestiges of collegiality in faculty government....departments—in the larger institutions—themselves embrace so many different specialists who are unable to communicate with one another."[50] Furthermore, "one of the problems of promoting cross-faculty and even intra-departmental collegiality even at the grassroots levels [is] the practical logistical difficulty of communication in a large university with many buildings and many sites"[51] More insidious complications to collegial process are found in the psychological dynamics wrapped up in the phenomenon of groupthink. The term "groupthink" was originally coined by Irving Janis at Yale University to describe "a mode of thinking that people engage in when they are deeply involved in a cohesive in-group, when the members' strivings for unanimity override their motivation to realistically appraise alternative courses of action."[52] Indeed, under certain circumstances, "preoccupation with agreement may distract group members from accomplishing the group's task."[53]

Proposals for preventing groupthink have been offered[54], but where groupthink is overcome, another psychological dynamic may take its place. Research indicates that even in settings designed for collegial decision making, it is "possible for vocal and articulate individuals to sway the decision-making process so that apparently collegial decisions" are actually "driven by [individuals with] their own agendas."[55] Finally, "from a purely practical point of view group decisions ordinarily require more time to make; they are ill adapted to emergencies or to situations requiring speed of decision, for one recalcitrant can delay decision making interminably."[56]

Collegial ideals wither in a world where "different people want different things and not everyone can have everything he or she desires. Different people have different identities, and their different definitions of appropriate behavior are mutually inconsistent."[57] Too often, the descriptive power of the collegial model pales in the face of "the real shape of governance at any university."[58]

The Anarchical (Garbage Can) Decision Making Model

Finally, the garbage can model portrays organizational decision making as an environment where the descriptive range of models based on intentional rationality, savvy politics, systematic bureaucracy, or good willed collegiality is inadequate. Instead,

> [O]rder emerges from the random interaction of problems, solutions, choice situations, and participants, rather than from intentions, plans, and consistent decisions. Timing and participation can shape outcomes. Managers' decisions can be influenced by people with whom they happen to be meeting, pressure to address problems that are thrust suddenly into the spotlight, windows of opportunity that can be linked with an existing problem and the existence of a pet solution.[59]

It is the overriding influence of an essentially serendipitous interaction of variables, as in a garbage can, that distinguishes this model from the others. The weight of the variables and their eventual effects can neither be thoroughly identified in advance, nor fully controlled at any point. Though hindsight can make some sense of how a decision took place, the variables change with each iteration and the new mix is no more predictable or controllable than the former mix. Indeed, "the worlds that confront decision makers appear to be systematically less orderly, more ambiguous, and more symbolic" than portrayed by standard decision making models.[60]

The "garbage can" metaphor can be traced to the definitive—now legendary—article for this model by Stanford researchers Michael Cohen and James March with University of Bergen professor Johan Olsen.[61] In addition, in his groundbreaking study of the federal government, University of Michigan political scientist John Kingdon masterfully demonstrated the transferability of the model to other settings.[62] Cohen et al. described universities as "organized anarchies" where individual decision makers are plagued by "problematic preferences, unclear technology, and fluid participation."[63]

First, decision maker preferences are described as "problematic" because an organized anarchy operates "on the basis of a variety of inconsistent and ill-defined preferences" and "it discovers preferences through action more than it acts on the basis of preferences."[64] And, "even when participants do define their preferences with a modicum of precision, they conflict."[65] The phenomenon of problematic preferences stands in sharp contrast to the assumptions of the rational decision making model.

Decision makers also operate in an environment overshadowed by "unclear technology." Writing in 1972, Cohen et al. meant technology in the sense of administrative mechanisms, not merely computer based tools. In the context of the early twenty-first century, however, advanced administrative computer systems—insofar as they mirror and extend administrative mechanisms—intensify the "unclear technology" with which decision makers contend. Technology is unclear insofar as an organization's "own processes are not understood by its members. It operates on the basis of simple trial-and-error procedures, the residue of learning from the accidents of past experience, and pragmatic inventions of necessity."[66] As put by Kingdon, "members have only fragmentary and rudimentary understandings of…how their jobs fit into a more general picture of the organization."[67] Unclear technology and the bureaucratic model are mutually exclusive.

Decision makers are also "fluid" participants in the decision making process: "participants vary in the amount of time and effort they devote to different domains; involvement varies from one time to another… audiences and decision makers for any particular kind of choice change capriciously."[68] This wreaks havoc on any attempt to calculate the power equation under a political decision making model, for "who shows up for or is invited to a given critical meeting, and their degree of activity at the meeting, for instance, turn out to make a tremendous difference."[69]

In this context, where decision makers are plagued with problematic preferences, unclear technology, and fluid participation, the garbage can model portrays multiple, largely *independent,* "streams" that flow through the organization. Cohen et al. named four streams: problems, solutions, participants, and choice opportunities.[70]

First is the **problem stream,** the aggregate of concerns held by people linked to the organization. Though these concerns directly affect the decision process, they are not necessarily genetically related to organizational goals: "they might arise over issues of lifestyle; family; frustrations of work; careers; group relations within the organization; distribution of status, jobs, and money; ideology; or current crises of mankind as interpreted by the mass media or the next door neighbor."[71]

Every problem occupies a span of time, requires a measure of energy, and competes for available solutions.

Second is the **solution stream:** "a solution is somebody's product" so, for instance, "a computer is not just a solution to a problem…it is an answer actively looking for a question."[72] Thus, solutions on a quest for problems to resolve circulate through the organization until they find—or fabricate—a problem to annex. Consequently, decision makers often "have fixed on a course of action and cast about for a problem to which it is the solution, discarding problems that don't seem to fit."[73]

Third is the **participant stream.** The level of participation from each individual ebbs and flows in relation to competing demands on time, energy, and interests. Participants themselves enter and exit due to extraneous circumstances. Finally, participants are not neutral, objective agents. They bring with them "issues and feelings looking for decision situations in which they might be aired."[74]

Fourth is the stream of **choice opportunities:** "These are occasions when and organization is expected to produce behavior that can be called a decision;" choice opportunities "arise regularly and any organization has ways of declaring an occasion for choice." A choice opportunity *is* the garbage can where problems, solutions, and eligible participants coincide to produce a decision: "choices are made only when the shifting combinations of problems, solutions, and decision makers happen to make action possible."[75]

Each of the streams influences decision outcomes (a) by affecting the time pattern of the arrival of problems, solutions, or decision makers, (b) by determining the allocation of energy by potential participants in the decision, and (c) by establishing linkages among the various streams.[76] In this model, organizational structure has less status than in the bureaucratic model. Here the structure may *influence* decision outcomes, but it cannot guarantee any particular outcome because of the effects of hidden undercurrents and shadow structures.

Decision Making Literature Review Summary

A common feature of the literature on each of the above five models is the balance between normative and descriptive applications.[77] The normative application of a model asserts that the features of the model *ought* to be consciously applied in the decision making process. A descriptive application attempts to observe how decision making actually takes place. The rational, bureaucratic, and collegial models are most frequently applied in a normative sense, though some of the literature seeks to show how these models provide strong descriptive insights. The political model is most often offered as a descriptive tool, though some normative applications are also available. The garbage can model was proposed by Cohen et al. as a purely descriptive model, and the literature seems to be void of arguments for its use as a normative guide for how decisions ought to be made.

Another tension in the literature is the presence of each type of phenomena—rational, bureaucratic, collegial, political, garbage can—in every decision setting. Each model struggles to account for this. Some scholars attempt a resolution by proposing pluralistic approaches to analysis, even offering cross comparison charts to enable linkage along various features.[78] The garbage can model, while accounting for the phenomena of the other models, is not an attempt at pluralism. Instead, it offers a separate unifying construct with all the descriptive power the other models together can claim. It demonstrates many of the strengths of the other models and few of their weaknesses. Under this model, organizational decision making is seen as

> an ecology of actors trying to act rationally with limited knowledge and preference coherence; trying to discover and execute proper behavior in ambiguous situations; and trying to discover, construct, and communicate interpretations of a confusing world.[79]

Thus, whereas other models look at strands of institutional life (the political, the bureaucratic, etc.), the garbage can model comes closest to a lens for viewing the weave of institutional life.

Conceptual Framework For This Study: The Garbage Can Model

The earliest decision making theories have been traced to the late eighteenth century work of economist Jeremy Bentham.[80] These theories relied on a definition of "economic man" that included assumptions that he is "completely informed" and "rational." As for being completely informed, "economic man is assumed to know not only what all the courses of action open to him are, but also what the outcome of any action will be."[81] Rationality, "the crucial fact about economic man," means that he is able to "order the states into which he can get, and he makes his choices so as to maximize something."[82]

By the mid-twentieth century, however, "economists and a few psychologists [had] produced a large body of theory and a few experiments that [dealt] with individual decision making."[83] In light of this, it was "easy for a psychologist to point out that an economic man who has [these] properties is very unlike a real man" and even economists had become "somewhat distrustful of economic man" and "worried" over assumptions related to his rationality.[84]

These doubts about the rationality of economic man were more fully explored in the writings of economist Herbert A. Simon. Simon believed that "decision making processes hold the key to the understanding of organizational phenomena."[85] He began writing in the 1940s and in 1978 he won the Nobel Prize in Economics "for his contribution to our understanding of decision making, particularly in organizations, and for numerous other contributions to social science."[86] That same year James March commended Simon, noting that it was a

> tribute to the power of Simon's intellect that this man whose most unwavering characteristic is a commitment to the intelligence of rational discourse and to the technology of reason, should receive the Nobel Prize for his provocative explication of some of the ways in which human beings and human institutions are often intelligent without being, in the usual sense, rational.[87]

Research with a provenance in Simon's ideas offers elements of a conceptual framework suitable to the study of decision making in a university setting.

One of the best known scholars in the Simon tradition is James G. March.[88] A text titled *Organizations* they coauthored in 1958 is still in print. March also coauthored another text with Richard M. Cyert.[89] These two works are considered "landmarks in the field of organizational theory."[90]

The research for this book relies on the garbage can model originally developed by March in collaboration with Cohen and Olsen[91] and adapted by Kingdon.[92] This model is particularly suited to the focus of this research since the focus of the original article adapted the conceptual insights of Simon and others to the university context. The garbage can model adaptation and, in fact, redevelopment by John Kingdon pictures multiple, largely independent, "streams" flowing through an organization: problems, solutions, participants, and choice opportunities. But the organization as a whole, as well as its members, are plagued by complex ambiguity: inconsistent preferences and priorities, stop-and-go time and attention, and transient decision making participation, all in the midst of shifting situations and contexts. In the words of Cohen et al.: "if the implications of the model are applicable anywhere, they are applicable to a university."[93]

Kingdon, in his adaption of the garbage can model to the study of federal health and transportation policy making in the United States, modified some of the terminology and identified corollary features of decision making processes that are easily grafted back into the original framework of Cohen et al. Kingdon's phenomena—such as policy entrepreneurs, focusing events, symbols, and spillover—add to the descriptive power of the original model.

Furthermore, the potential contribution of this model to understanding the use of technology forecasts in decision making is highlighted by the competing rational model prevalent in the technology planning literature leading up to the 1990s: "at their core, the assumptions and premises underlying current [1980s information technology] planning literature and practice assume a rational model of organizational decision processes."[94] The approach of a text on decision making methodology for information technology investment, written in 2004, echoes the same rational model assumptions:

> to make good decisions on information technology today requires [the ability] to integrate the complexity of decision criteria in such a way that a decision choice is clear and clearly supported by the analysis.... Information technology decisions must be supported by comprehensive inclusion of all relevant decision-making criteria.[95]

If "technology devices are not neutral information tools, as some administrators might think"[96] and if "technology helps steer the organizational assumptions of institutions"[97] then a test of the garbage can model in relation to decision making in the light of technology forecasts has potential for developing insight into what is sometimes a gear grinding experience. As put by Cohen and March: "the great advantage of trying to see garbage can phenomena together as a process is the possibility that…decision making can take account of its existence, and that, to some extent, it can be managed."[98]

How do library directors and other key decision making participants describe decision making during the construction of new academic libraries? This is the bellwether question for the conceptual framework of this research. Since library directors are the conventional locus for decision making during the construction of new academic libraries, their perspectives were central to this study. The garbage can model suggests, however, that the process is not as simple as this. Data analysis was, therefore, sensitive to the presence of other loci for decision making.

Conclusion

Technology rarely—if ever—yields lasting benefits without first taking us through a maze of starts, stops, and unanticipated forks. Furthermore, standard decision making models do not adequately account for the fact that large scale institutional decision making takes us through the same maze and is plagued by ambiguity, inconsistency, shifting situations, and transient decision making participation.

Since decision making involves assumptions about the future, technology advocates are adept at positioning themselves in our future by offering luminous forecasts about their products. The use of a clear technology forecast to reduce the existential tension of uncertainty about the future may seem to offer an anchor point for decision making in the sea of ambiguity. But as chapter 3 will show, technology forecasts are particularly susceptible to bias, ideological servitude, and political manipulation.

Notes

1. Gore and Silander, "A Bibliographical Essay on Decision Making," 121.
2. On July 11, 2007, fully 124,768 unduplicated items—nearly twenty-five times more than Gore and Silander's "large body of literature"—appeared under the subject of decision making from a single cross index EBSCO Host search of Academic Search Premier, Business Source Premier, ERIC, PsychINFO, SocINDEX with

Full Text, and Library, Information Science & Technology Abstracts. On August 18, 2007, a federated search of 108 databases provided by the Thomas Cooper Library at the University of South Carolina produced 853,141 items under the subject of decision making. Though the federated search contains duplicated items, it nevertheless illustrates the vast attention paid to this topic in the literature.

3. Payne, "The Scarecrow's Search: A Cognitive Psychologist's Perspective on Organizational Decision Making," 354.
4. Chaffee, *Rational Decision Making in Higher Education*, 5.
5. Baldridge, *Power and Conflict in the University: Research in the Sociology of Complex Organizations*, 9.
6. Cohen, March, and Olsen, "A Garbage Can Model of Organizational Choice."
7. Chaffee, *Rational Decision Making in Higher Education*, 2.
8. Ibid., 5, 6.
9. e.g.: Caldwell, "Bureaucratic Foreign Policy Making;" Huber, "The Nature of Organizational Decision Making and the Design of Decision Support Systems;" Hickson, "Decision Making at the Top of Organizations;" Hoy and Tartar, *Administrators Solving the Problems of Practice: Decision-making Concepts, Cases, and Consequences.*
10. Plous, *The Psychology of Judgment and Decision Making*, 77.
11. Schmidt, "Executive Decision Making," 103.
12. Etzioni, "Guidance Rules and Rational Decision Making," 758.
13. Kepner and Tregoe, *The Rational Manager: A Systematic Approach to Problem Solving and Decision Making*, 39.
14. Gore, Murray, and Richardson, *Strategic Decision Making*, 5–7.
15. Simon, "Administrative Decision Making," 33.
16. Tversky and Shafir, "The Disjunction Effect in Choice Under Uncertainty," 305.
17. Herrnstein, "Rational Choice Theory: Necessary But Not Sufficient," 356.
18. Ehrenberg, "In Pursuit of University Wide Objectives," 29.
19. Jones, *Politics and the Architecture of Choice: Bounded Rationality and Governance*, 45.
20. Augier, "James March on Education, Leadership, and Don Quixote: Introduction and Interview," 170.
21. Oliver Marnet of the University of Bath surveyed the scholarly literature in a 2007 article and concluded: "the assumption that people will actually behave in ways" predicted by rational choice models "is at odds with a large body of evidence from psychology and behavioral research" (Marnet, "History Repeats Itself: The Failure of Rational Choice Models in Corporate Governance," 195.)
22. Ibid., 205.
23. Plous, *The Psychology of Judgment and Decision Making*, 13.
24. Beach and Connolly, *The Psychology of Decision Making: People in Organizations*, 2nd ed., 125.
25. Brockhoff, "Decision Quality and Information;" Hall, Ariss, and Todorov, "The Illusion of Knowledge: When More Information Reduces Accuracy and Increases Confidence."
26. e.g. Gore, Murray, and Richardson, *Strategic Decision Making.*
27. See especially Tversky and Kahneman, "Rational Choice and the Framing of Decisions," where they conclude that "deviations of actual behavior from the [rational

model] are too widespread to be ignored, too systematic to be dismissed as random error, and too fundamental to be accommodated by relaxing the normative system" (252).

28. Baldridge, *Power and Conflict in the University: Research in the Sociology of Complex Organizations*, 23.

29. Pfeffer, *Managing With Power: Politics and Influence in Organizations*, 71.

30. Salancik and Pfeffer, "The Bases and Use of Power in Organizational Decision Making: The Case of a University," 454.

31. Dimaggio and Powell, "The Iron Cage Revisited: Institutional Isomorphism and Collective Rationality in Organizational Fields," 157.

32. Wood, "Power Relationships and Group Decision Making in Organizations," 280.

33. March, *A Primer on Decision Making: How Decisions Happen*, 143.

34. Childers, "What is Political About Bureaucratic-Collegial Decision Making?"

35. Weber, *The Theory of Social and Economic Organization*, 337.

36. Weber, *From Max Weber: Essays in Sociology*, 196.

37. Huber, "The Nature of Organizational Decision Making and the Design of Decision Support Systems," 4.

38. Glueck and Dennis, "Bureaucratic, Democratic and Environmental Approaches to Organizational Design," 201–202.

39. Caldwell, "Bureaucratic Foreign Policy Making," 95.

40. Boseman and McAlpine, "Goals and Bureaucratic Decision Making: An Experiment," 418.

41. Fincher, "On the Rational Solution of Dominant Issues in Higher Education," 492.

42. Baldridge et al., "Alternative Models of Governance in Higher Education," 36.

43. Meister-Scheytt and Scheytt, "The Complexity of Change in Universities," 88.

44. Baylis, *Governing by Committee: Collegial Leadership in Advanced Societies*, 7.

45. Ibid.

46. Childers, "What is Political About Bureaucratic-Collegial Decision Making?" 26.

47. Baldridge, *Power and Conflict in the University: Research in the Sociology of Complex Organizations*, 11.

48. Buchanan and O'Connell, "A Brief History of Decision Making," 36.

49. Baylis, *Governing by Committee: Collegial Leadership in Advanced Societies*, 1.

50. McConnell, "Faculty Government," 100.

51. Hellawell and Hancock, "A Case Study of the Changing Role of the Academic Middle Manager in Higher Education: Between Hierarchical Control and Collegiality?," 183–187.

52. Buchanan and O'Connell, "A Brief History of Decision Making," 37.

53. Rawlins, "Consensus in Decision-Making Groups: A Conceptual History," 33.

54. e.g., Hart, "Preventing Groupthink: Evaluating and Reforming Groups in Government."

55. Hellawell and Hancock, "A Case Study," 187.

56. McMurry, "The Case for Benevolent Autocracy," 85.

57. March, *A Primer on Decision Making*, 106.

58. Baldridge, *Power and Conflict in the University: Research in the Sociology of Complex Organizations*, 11.

59. Barry, Cramton, and Carroll, "Navigating the Garbage Can: How Agendas Help Managers Cope With Job Realities," 27.
60. March, *A Primer on Decision Making*, 175.
61. Cohen, March, and Olsen, "A Garbage Can Model of Organizational Choice."
62. Kingdon, *Agendas, Alternatives, and Public Policies.*
63. Cohen et al., "A Garbage Can Model, of Organizational Choice," 1.
64. Ibid.
65. Kingdon, *Agendas, Alternatives, and Public Policies*, 84.
66. Cohen et al., "A Garbage Can Model, of Organizational Choice," 1.
67. Kingdon, *Agendas, Alternatives, and Public Policies*, 84.
68. Cohen et al., "A Garbage Can Model, of Organizational Choice," 1.
69. Kingdon, *Agendas, Alternatives, and Public Policies*, 84.
70. Cohen et al., "A Garbage Can Model, of Organizational Choice," 3; Kingdon named three streams that coincide with the first three streams from Cohen et al.: "problems, policies, politics" (Kingdon, *Agendas, Alternatives, and Public Policies*, 201).
71. Cohen et al., "A Garbage Can Model, of Organizational Choice," 3.
72. Ibid.
73. Kingdon, *Agendas, Alternatives, and Public Policies*, 86.
74. Cohen et al., "A Garbage Can Model, of Organizational Choice," 2.
75. Ibid., 16.; Though Kingdon does not name this fourth stream, this description matches his exposition on "coupling," i.e., "a joining of all three streams" that "dramatically enhances the odds that a subject will become firmly fixed on a decision agenda" (Kingdon, *Agendas, Alternatives*, 202).
76. Ibid., 4.
77. Slovic, Fischhoff and Lichtenstein, "Behavioral Decision Theory."
78. e.g., Bolman and Deal, *Reframing Organizations: Artistry, Choice, and Leadership.*
79. March, "How Decisions Happen in Organizations," 111.
80. Edwards, "The Theory of Decision Making."
81. Ibid., 381.
82. Ibid.
83. Ibid., 380..
84. Ibid., 382, 411.
85. Simon, *Administrative Behavior: A Study of Decision-Making Processes in Administrative Organization*, xl.
86. March, "The 1978 Nobel Peace Prize in Economics," 858.
87. Ibid. March further notes that Simon's work "initiated a string of related developments by others that have come collectively to be called a theory of limited, or bounded, rationality" (859) and according to Kahneman "the concept of bounded rationality…defines the problem that the field has been trying to solve ever since [Simon first introduced it]" (Kahneman, "Judgment and Decision Making: A Personal View," 142).
88. The ongoing influence of March can be seen through a combined search of Science Citation Index, Social Sciences Citation Index, and Arts & Humanities Citation Index. A search for March as an author or coauthor returns 164 publications. These publications are cited 6,231 times in scholarly literature and one stands out with 917 citations: "A Garbage Can Model of Organizational Choice."

89. Cyert and March, *A Behavioral Theory of the Firm*.
90. Shapira, "Introduction and Overview," 4.
91. Cohen et al., "A Garbage Can Model of Organizational Choice."
92. Kingdon, *Agendas, Alternatives, and Public Policies*.
93. Cohen et al., "A Garbage Can Model of Organizational Choice," 11.
94. Boynton and Zmud, "Information Technology Planning for the 1990's: Directions for Practice and Research," 58.
95. Schniederjans, Hamaker, and Schniederjans, *Information Technology Investment: Decision-making Methodology*, vii.
96. Sellers, "Moogle, Google, and Garbage Cans: The Impact of Technology on Decision Making," 370.
97. Macpherson, "Escaping to Technology-based Faculty Development: A Case for Reforming Professional Development in a Knowledge Organization," 275.
98. Cohen and March, *Leadership and Ambiguity: The American College President*, 91.

CHAPTER THREE

Technology Forecasts:
Caveat Emptor

Decision making involves assumptions about the future. Technology advocates speak with confidence about technology and its place in the future. But technology forecasting has an unusually weak history of success, weaker than even most advocates know. This has implications for how forecasts are used in decision making.

"We have before us the technological possibility of freeing mankind from drudgery, providing mankind with incalculable material abundance, and giving humanity the leisure time to develop its full potentialities." ~ *1954 statement on machine automation*[1]

"The great paradox of our age is that, while more and more people enjoy the benefits of technological and economic growth, increasing numbers of people are poor, unhealthy, and lack access to education." ~ *2006 "update on the state of the future"*[2]

Introduction

Technology can yield amazing results but usually not without taking us through a confusing maze. Large scale institutional decision making takes us through the same maze and when technology is in the mix, the process sprouts new twists and turns. Decision making involves assumptions about the future and attractive forecasts—especially technology forecasts—are sometimes used to reduce a sense of uncertainty and confusion by speaking with clarity in the midst of ambiguity. But technology forecasts are particularly susceptible to being unreliable anchor points for decision making.

This research explores the process of decision making during the construction of new academic libraries at American universities, with special attention to the influence of technological forecasting as a subtopic of all decision making during the construction process.[3] The years leading up to the construction of these libraries are of particular interest because they included some of the most dramatic technological developments in recent history: the introduction of the internet, the development of the world wide web, and the aftermath of the dot-com stock market bubble.

Forecasting has been applied to higher education to predict everything from its imminent demise to the dawning of a new era. The use of technology in an increasingly diffuse set of higher education activities, from payroll to pedagogy, has engendered a distinct body of literature devoted to forecasts of the impact of technology on colleges and universities.[4] Publications on this topic, covering every conceivable aspect of higher education, appear as early as 1910. Publication volume, however, is heavily skewed toward the most recent twenty years: more citations appear in the years 1990-2009 than in the previous 79 years combined.

Persuasive forecasts have the power to shape decision making related to the deployment of large amounts of human, capital, and physical resources. One prominent example occurred during the 1990s when some library building projects were attenuated and print collections were mothballed based on forecasts that physical space and print collections would soon drop into insignificance due to the looming all digital environment.

Forecasting has drawn the attention of numerous disciplines. Psychologists, anthropologists, historians, and social critics have produced literature on forecasting as a subject of study. Observations from these fields suggest that a forecast is not merely a forecast. Instead, it is often a complex mix of subjective dynamics offered as a simplified set of "objective" propositions. Studies by psychologists and the observations of social critics are especially instructive in this regard.

The Psychology of Forecasting

Psychologists examined prediction behavior as early as 1938.[5] In that year Hadley Cantril of Princeton University—writing in the *Journal of Abnormal and Social Psychology*—reported research that found that the content of a prediction can be an expression of wish fulfillment[6], that "individuals whose attitudes favor a certain outcome for an event, tend to forecast the desired outcome"[7], and that when people make predictions related to internalized social values, ego involvement (bias driven by personal preferences, interests and goals) can become a determining factor.[8] Also in 1938, Douglas McGregor of MIT concluded that personality traits such as optimism and pessimism, skepticism and cautiousness, exert a strong influence on the predictive process.[9]

More recent research on the heuristics of intuitive predictions suggests that strictly intuitive predictions are characterized by "unjustified confidence" and are "insensitive to the reliability of the evidence or to the prior probability of the outcome" leading people to "erroneously predict rare events and extreme values."[10] Forecasting is, it seems, plagued by multiple, incompatible sets of variables. What we anticipate—and so what we are disposed to forecast—is more an expression of "ideology, profession, region, religion, and culture"[11] yet the accuracy of a forecast is dependent upon a disaggregation of these factors from the process[12], a difficult—likely impossible—task. We are left with the observation of University of Pittsburg philosophy professor Nicholas Rescher: "often as not, futuristic speculation tells us more about futurists than about the future."[13] Indeed, in the vocabulary of the Garbage Can decision making model, a forecast is a solution—real or fabricated, it matters not—looking for a problem to annex.

Thus, a forecast is a construct. The traits of a construct as described by famed researchers Egon Guba and Yvonna Lincoln are notably similar to psychologists' observations about forecasts: they are formed to make sense of situations, they are shaped by the values of the individual forming the construct, and they "are inextricably linked to the particular physical, psychological, social, and cultural contexts within which they are formed and to which they refer."[14]

Social Criticism of Forecasting

Though social criticism is not a specialized scholarly discipline, commentary from this perspective is relevant to an understanding of forecasting behavior in a broader sense, especially in light of how it complements the findings of psychologists.[15] As noted by Max Dublin, "predicting the future has become so integral to the fabric of modern consciousness that few people feel compelled to question it, and fewer still feel the need to defend it."[16] But Dublin further notes that forecasts are powerful rhetorical and propaganda devices: "predictions do not simply describe the world—they *act* on it.…predictions are seldom neutral, seldom merely descriptive. [They] are also prescriptive; they contain a strong element of advice and warning."[17] In addition to serving as a propaganda device, Dublin describes forecasting as "a basic tool of ideology"—ideological battles are often waged on the basis of ideologically scripted, self-serving forecasts.[18]

Library Dean Mark Herring observed that "for Americans, technology is one of the highest expressions of our greatness and we adore it with studied pride".[19] In his critique of technology forecasting, CUNY marketing professor Steven Schnaars spoke of how "technological wonder" affects the process of making a forecast. Forecasters under the influence of technological wonder "fall in love with the technology…and ignore the market the technology is intended to serve. The forecasters are blinded by their emotions and lose perspective of commonsense economic considerations."[20] As a result, according to Schnaars, the forecaster uncritically assumes "that consumers will find the new technology as enticing and irresistible as they do."[21]

Forecasting Methods

Numerous forecasting methods have been devised; one text from 1975 lists 150.[22] The most common forecasting methods in higher education settings are trend extrapolation, expert forecasting, and scenario development.

Trend Extrapolation

Futurist Theodore Gordon has observed that "most people, most of the time, forecast by extrapolating trends."[23] This forecasting method "consists of the extension of historical and present patterns into the future."[24] Trend extrapolation assumes a methodical evolutionary process, a "continuous, linear, unidirectional movement from past to present to future, without the intervention of surprises or crises."[25] But, as Gordon cautioned, trend extrapolation "is bound to be wrong eventually. Simply extending historical trends into the future is easy, but this process suggests that nothing new will deflect the trends, that the only forces shaping the future are those that existed in the past."[26]

For instance, Ray Kurzweil was speaking in terms of trend extrapolation when he wrote

> The virtual book was introduced in the early 1990s and…has already demonstrated a superiority to the paper-based technology in certain categories. As we go through the 1990s, virtual books will undergo an evolution that will see 500-year-old print into obsolescence by the end of the decade.[27]

True to the method, Kurzweil's prediction did not consider the possible intervention of, for instance, technical or economic surprises.

Expert Forecasting

This method is a simply a matter of a single authority making "explicit guesstimates about the future."[28] Used with discretion, this method provides a plausible starting point but should be supplemented with careful analysis by others.[29] This method has also been called "genius" forecasting.[30] But true genius forecasting "requires one ingredient that is difficult to obtain: a genius."[31] The attraction of expert forecasting is its rational model of decision making ambience. But on closer examination, expert forecasting is actually an "intuitive" approach marked by "pronounced fallibility."[32]

A subcategory of the genius forecast might be named "celebrity" forecasting. By way of example, during the rapid expansion of the internet during the 1990s, many "genius" forecasts were made by celebrities with "genius" status garnered from sudden success as internet entrepreneurs rather than from technical or educational credentials. In celebrity forecasts, informed opinions offered by individuals with expertise are supplanted by scenarios offered by individuals with celebrity status.

Scenario Development

A scenario is "an account or synopsis of a possible course of action or events."[33] Whereas simple trend extrapolation is linear and deemphasizes the intervention of surprises, the use of scenarios is an "attempt to integrate individual analyses of trends and potential events into a holistic picture of the future…to provide for, and describe, the interaction of these trends and events; and ultimately, to explore the possible course of alternative futures."[34] Scenario development is most useful when multiple scenarios are considered:

> …multiple scenarios force those involved in planning to put aside personal perspectives and to consider the possibility of other futures predicated on value sets that may not otherwise be articulated. Grappling with different scenarios also compels the user to deal explicitly with the cause-and-effect relationships of selected events and trends. Thus, multiple scenarios give a primary role to human judgment, the most useful and least well used factor in the planning process. Scenarios therefore provide a useful context in which planning discussions may take place and provide those within the college or university a shared frame of reference concerning the future.[35]

Since trends and potential events do not remain static, "scenarios should be re-evaluated and revised on a regular basis."[36] Though published re-evaluations of previously articulated scenarios are not common, one example is found in articles in 2001 and 2003 by Mick O'Leary. In 2001 O'Leary offered scenarios related to the development of ebook technology.[37] In 2003, he re-evaluated those scenarios and commented on elements worth reemphasizing as well as elements requiring revision.[38] Librarians have published articles related to scenario development and collection development,[39] the "library of the future,"[40] reference services,[41] and retention of print serial subscriptions.[42]

Technology Forecasts and Higher Education

Despite the profound foibles intrinsic to forecasting, decision makers are shackled with the predicament that

> A key aspect of any decision making situation is being able to predict the circumstances that surround that decision and that situation. Such predictions, generally handled under the title of forecasting, have been identified as a key subpart of the decision making process.[43]

Forecasting is intrinsic to decision making, whether conceived as such or not.

This is especially true with decision making related to technology. As put by one college administrator, "a college's future is tied to technology, and decisions are tied to technology's output. Response to needs and decisions about alternatives are tied to how much emphasis is placed upon technology to aid administrators toward their goals."[44] As with forecasts in general, forecasts anticipating the impact of technology on higher education address virtually every aspect of university life. The few short illustrations below manage to touch on facilities, pedagogy, libraries, tenure, accreditation, finance, and governance.

In 1997 management guru Peter Drucker predicted that "thirty years from now the big university campuses will be relics. Universities won't survive. It's as large a change as when we got the printed book."[45] Drucker's support for this prediction involved the impact of technology: "Already we are beginning to deliver more lectures and classes off campus via satellite or two-way video at a fraction of the cost. The college won't survive as a residential institution. Today's buildings are hopelessly unsuited and totally unneeded."[46]

One year later, in 1998, Brian Hawkins of EDUCAUSE and former University Librarian at Columbia University Patricia Battin compiled a sweeping collection of essays to "confront the issues surrounding the transformation of academic institutions by digital technology."[47] Within these essays, computer centers, media units, instructional technology services, and libraries receive special attention through the lens of a conviction that discontinuity with the past—revolution—is the only way to avoid collapse of our academic institutions. An EDUCAUSE publication titled *Dancing With the Devil* further warned that

> The application of new technologies to postsecondary education creates a significant likelihood that new players—those without fixed investments in physical plants or tenured professors—will obtain accreditation and will compete with traditional colleges and universities in a number of markets...This possibility has the potential to change U.S. higher education in profound ways.[48]

Echoing these thoughts, a 2002 document from the National Research Council predicted that "The impact of information technology on the research university will likely be profound, rapid, and discontinuous… technology will not only transform the intellectual activities of the research university but will also change how the university is organized, financed, and governed."[49]

The themes of "rapid," "discontinuous," "emergent," and "disruptive" permeate the terms and tone of mainstream forecasts regarding the impact of technology on higher education. Such forecasts rouse a sense of urgency, even of crisis. At a minimum, perceived urgency and crisis will affect decision making by shortening the time frame given to the process. In decision making situations involving complex and sometimes confusing variables, such as with sophisticated technological applications, less time for thought and reflection is not likely to have a neutral bearing. In addition, the amount of time given to the forecasting task may affect the forecasting method of choice. Methods that demand less time, effort, and sophistication may be chosen in greater proportion simply on the basis of time and resource constraints instead of on the basis of reasoned conclusions about the appropriateness of a particular method to a particular task.

The predictions noted in this section illustrate how forecasts can have significant implications related to decision making. When Drucker predicted that the residential college will not survive, the "residential versus remote" educational models are tacitly engaged, ideological frameworks behind each approach are evoked, and decisions to carry us along one path or another beckon. When Hawkins and Battin declared that discontinuity with the past is the only way to avoid collapse of our academic institutions, a course of decision making—one that establishes discontinuity with the past—is unavoidably implied. Finally, when the National Research Council declared that the effects of information technology "will likely be profound, rapid, and discontinuous" and "technology will not only transform the intellectual activities of the research university but will also change how the university is organized, financed, and governed," decision making to accommodate these claims is invited.

Technology Forecasts and Academic Libraries

Libraries have been progressive implementers of technology for centuries. During the twentieth century, as academic libraries became increasingly technology intensive, forecasts about the impact of technology in higher education naturally included projections relating to the library. In times of rapid change, the consequences of decisions about technology are heightened by heavy costs and accelerated obsolescence cycles. During such times, technology forecasts may seem to take on greater importance but they also accrue greater ambiguity. The volume of forecasting literature in the last two decades suggests that we are in a time of uniquely rapid change. Sweeping change, rapid technological developments, and uncertainty have combined to engender a steady stream of library related forecasts.

More than twenty years ago, George Keller of the University of Pennsylvania spoke of rapid change, "the technological imperative," and the importance of technology forecasts:

> The rapid growth of electronic technology in the past two decades presents universities with the first major transformation in the transmission and storage of ideas and information since the introduction of printing in fifteenth-century Italy and Germany. It is an absolutely shattering development…[50]

Keller further noted that "new technology is altering the college library as we have known it for centuries."[51]

Keller's observations are based on the 1960s and 1970s, but similar comments appear again and again through the years. In 1990, James Morrison of UNC-Chapel Hill noted that "we are living in exciting times, with unprecedented changes occurring in the world around us. Consequently, our institutions of higher education are faced with a complex, turbulent, and uncertain future."[52] In 1992, Carol Hughes echoes this in an article in the *Journal of Academic Librarianship:* "Research libraries are facing an unprecedented rate of change as the year 2000 approaches, much of which is being brought about by developments in information technology."[53] Looking back on a technology that was new in the 1990s (the internet), Patricia Breivik and Gordon Gee observed in a 2006 publication for the American Council on Education that "the academic environment has been unalterably changed by the presence of the internet."[54]

By 2007, it was possible for David Lewis to conclude in an article for *College & Research Libraries* that

> The wide application of digital technologies to scholarly communications has disrupted the model of academic library service that has been in place for the past century. Given the new Internet tools and the explosive growth of digital content available on the Web, it is now not entirely clear what an academic library should be.[55]

The perceived pace of change shows no sign of abatement. During times characterized by persistent change, insight regarding decision making processes can have increasingly far reaching implications. Furthermore, a fuller understanding of decision making related to technology can provide direction for professional practice among administrators, faculty, and librarians.

The stakes are high. There are nearly 3,500 academic libraries in the United States[56] engaging more than 136,000,000 circulation transactions per year.[57] Academic libraries in the United States hold 3.5 billion volumes[58] and spend $1,443,102,475 per year for new acquisitions.[59] Indeed, "the future has political as well as analytic consequences. Assumptions about it govern the management of resources at every level—domestic, national, global."[60] Decision making about libraries, and the forecasts these decisions imply, possess great power to influence the direction of library development, involving vast collections of human, capital, and physical resources.

Decision making about libraries also tacitly challenges or confirms conceptions of the purpose for libraries. The significance of a decision or a forecast is therefore broader than the stated subject of the decision or forecast. For example, according to Walt Crawford and Michael Gorman

> Libraries exist to acquire, give access to, and safeguard carriers of knowledge and information in all forms and to provide instruction and assistance in the use of the collections to which their users have access. In short, libraries exist to give meaning to the continuing human

attempt to transcend space and time in the advance-
ment of knowledge and the preservation of culture.[61]

So, for instance, the popular notion of a future where all libraries
are completely virtual requires a revision of Crawford and Gorman since
they state that libraries acquire all forms, not just digital. For a library
director contemplating the construction of a new library, whether or
not to make this kind of revision involves a *decision* about the *future* **and**
the purpose for libraries in that future. The importance of this point—as
illustrated in the research of Yale university librarian Scott Bennett—is
of great consequence.

Bennett notes that during the 1990s colleges and universities were
experiencing "at least two fundamental discontinuities with their past."[62]
The first involved an acknowledgement and engagement "with the
social dimensions of learning and knowledge."[63] The second, "a revolution in information technology, was not at all quiet and was even more
pervasive."[64] Both of these discontinuities bear heavily on "conceptions
of the library as a place."[65] How we envision the *purpose* of the library
shapes how—*or whether*—we plan for new physical library space: "Fun-
damentally, the choice before us is that between viewing the library as
an information repository on the one hand and as a learning enterprise
on the other."[66] The two conceptions are not mutually exclusive but the
question of which drives the decision making and planning process is
not inconsequential. Those who press for the library as a *digital* information repository jeopardize the known contributions that well articulated
physical space can make to the learning process.[67] On the other hand,
an overemphasis on the library as a *print* information repository can also
backfire: "Library after library has sacrificed reader accommodations
to the imperatives of shelving. The crowding out of readers by reading
matter is one of the most common and disturbing ironies in library
space planning. These outcomes must be acknowledged, in fact, to be
a failure in planning."[68]

For Bennett, "the general challenge for library space design" is
this: "Is it possible to design a library so that it functions as a powerful
learning space—one that encourages students to devote more time to
study—as well as an effective service space?"[69] He encourages us to be
"endlessly inventive in creating and celebrating the cultures of place in
academic life"[70] and to pay attention to "first questions"[71] that we keep

at the center of attention as we plan new learning spaces.

However conceived, the library remains a vital subsystem within the greater social system of higher education. No other institution in American culture, including higher education, is capable of fulfilling the historic role of the library. Libraries will persist as a vital cultural force in American higher education, and technology will continue to wield a formidable influence on the character of library—and university-wide—culture. In fact, insofar as libraries showcase many of the functions of the larger university setting (academic, administrative, physical plant, human resources, etc.) they may be viewed as a vital microcosm or exemplar of the larger university context. Their particular sensitivity to technological change makes them a rich case study for decision making with a focus on technology, a focus not unrelated to a concern for learning: "We face the challenge of internet-savvy students whose ease of use of on-line resources is not matched with critical judgment about the quality of those resources and whose understanding of research has often been shaped by technical expertise rather than critical questions."[72]

Brutal Facts About Forecasts

The literature suggests that the apparent pace of cultural change continues to increase. In a book of reflections on the twentieth century titled *Faster: The Acceleration of Just About Everything* James Gleick observed that "we are in a rush. We are making haste. A compression of time characterizes the life of the century now closing."[73] Stephen Bertman of the University of Windsor, in his book *Hyperculture: The Cost of Human Speed*, stated that "supported by an electronic network of instantaneous communications, our culture has been transformed into a 'synchronous society,' a nationally and globally integrated culture in which the prime and unchallenged directive is to keep up with change."[74] Cambridge trained engineer John Naughton wrote a book in 2000 with the title *A Brief History of the Future: From Radio Days to Internet Years in a Lifetime.*[75]

In this kind of environment, the stakes for academic libraries remain high, and the perceived need to anticipate the future is undiminished:

> Research libraries will continue to be affected by rapid
> and transformative changes in information technology
> and the networked environment for the foreseeable

future. The pace and direction of these changes will profoundly challenge libraries and their staffs to respond effectively.[76]

This is further illustrated by the fact that countless thousands of forecasts have been offered for higher education and academic libraries in recent decades.

The relentless cycle of new-newer-newest in the development of communications technologies has produced a steady flow of forecasts related to how these technologies could affect libraries. Differing opinions abound, but all share the view that the effects are far from neutral. As noted earlier, observations from various academic fields suggest that a forecast is not merely a forecast. Instead, a forecast is often a complex mix of favorite factoids and subjective dynamics offered as a simplified set of "objective" propositions. In light of this, several "brutal facts" about forecasts should be kept in mind.

Forecasts are unavoidable. Tacitly or explicitly, every decision presupposes a future state of affairs that will corroborate the terms of the decision and validate its credibility. Consequently, every decision *implies* a forecast; every forecast invites a decision.

Forecasts are not neutral. Decisions and the forecasts they imply can have significant implications in institutional settings. Consider the following observations: "what we do depends on what we expect to happen;"[77] decision makers "who do not look ahead…become prisoners of external forces and surprises, most of them unpleasant;"[78] "no long-range planning will have true validity unless the future is anticipated today;"[79] and "the future is at least in part what we make it" and part of planning is to "outline the future we want to have" and then to create it in the present.[80]

Forecasts are ideologically grounded: "forecasts are specifically useful in changing someone's view of what's going to happen, and therefore in influencing that person's thinking."[81] A forecaster can promote ideological change by making persuasive forecasts articulated in terms of the ideology. For instance, a university administrator who is committed to an ideology of technological diffusion can influence the thinking—and decision making—of others by shaping forecasts around evidence and suppositions that a state of technological diffusion is inevitable.

Forecasts are politically charged: "Some forecasts are particularly important since they have a 'cascading' effect; the initial forecast affects one decision which then has knock-on effects on a series of other related decisions."[82] Because of their power to affect decision making processes, forecasts can affect educational policy formation.[83] As it cascades, a forecast that affects decisions about policy formation can subsequently steer resource allocation and budgeting. The extent to which a forecast influences policy and budgeting decisions is a measure of its political power in the hands of a persuasive advocate.

Conclusion

Technology forecasts are not simple compass points for planning and decision making. The adoption and diffusion of new technology is never a clear cut process. Large scale institutional decision making—especially when it involves considerations of technology—is not always fully comprehensible *even to decision making participants*. But this is not a call nihilistic surrender. The next three chapters will show that within the complexity, unpredictability, and uncontrollability of institutional decision settings, general patterns can be discerned, opportunities may be realized, and meaningful progress is possible. Strikingly beautiful libraries—sources of immense benefit—now stand on each of the campuses studied for this research.

Notes

1. Cited in Asheim, *The Future of the Book*, 6.
2. Glenn and Gordon, "Update on the State of the Future," 21.
3. Keller listed five areas where forecasting is applied within higher education: technological, economic, demographic, politico-legal, and sociocultural (*Academic Strategy: The Management Revolution in American Higher Education,* 158).
4. The ERIC database produces more than 18,000 English language items for higher education forecasts [Boolean query (higher education AND (futures OR prediction OR trends)) using EBSCOHOST ERIC].
5. Cantril, "The Prediction of Social Events."; McGregor, "The Major Determinants of the Prediction of Social Events."
6. Cantril, "The Prediction of Social Events," 380.
7. Ibid., 387.
8. Ibid., 389.
9. McGregor, "The Major Determinants of the Prediction of Social Events."
10. Kahneman and Tversky, "On the Psychology of Prediction," 237.
11. Markley and McCuan, *America Beyond 2001: Opposing Viewpoints,* 12.
12. Loye, *The Knowable Future: A Psychology of Forecasting and Prophecy,* 13.

13. Rescher, *Predicting the Future: An Introduction to the Theory of Forecasting*, 28.
14. Guba and Lincoln, *Fourth Generation Evaluation*, 8.
15. Representatives of this approach include the following: Schnaars, *Megamistakes: Forecasting and the Myth of Rapid Technological Change*; Dublin, *Futurehype: The Tyranny of Prophecy*; Sherden, *The Fortune Sellers: The Big Business of Buying and Selling Predictions*; Sardar, *Rescuing all Our Futures: The Future of Future Studies*.
16. Dublin, *Futurehype: The Tyranny of Prophecy*, 1.
17. Ibid., 4.
18. Ibid., 12, 82, 83.
19. Herring, *Fool's Gold: Why the Internet is No Substitute for a Library*, 2.
20. Schnaars, *Megamistakes: Forecasting and the Myth of Rapid Technological Change*, 9, 10.
21. Ibid., 10.
22. Mitchell et al., *Handbook of Forecasting Techniques*, 285–292.
23. Gordon, "The Methods of Futures Research," 30.
24. Haas, *Future Studies in the K–12 Curriculum*, 41.
25. Ibid.
26. Gordon, "The Methods of Futures Research," 26.
27. Kurzweil, "The Virtual Library," 54.
28. Morrison et al., *Futures Research and the Strategic Planning Process*, 42.
29. Ibid., 43.
30. Martino, *Technological Forecasting for Decisionmaking*.
31. Gordon, "The Methods of Futures Research," 28.
32. Slocum and Lundberg, "Technology Forecasting: From Emotional to Empirical," 140.
33. Mish, ed., *Merriam-Webster's Collegiate Dictionary. 10*th ed. , 1043.
34. Wilson, "Scenarios," 228.
35. Morrison et al., *Futures Research and the Strategic Planning Process*, 76.
36. de Kock, "Using Scenarios in Planning a Digital Information Service," 54.
37. O'Leary, "Ebook Scenarios."
38. O'Leary, "Ebook Scenarios Updated."
39. Shuman, *The Library of the Future*.
40. Giesecke, "Scenario Planning and Collection Development."
41. Watstein, "Scenario Planning for the Future of Reference."
42. McDonald, "No One Uses Them So Why Should We Keep Them?"
43. Wheelright and Makridakis, *Forecasting Methods for Management*, 1.
44. Sellers, "Moogle, Google, and Garbage Cans," 373.
45. Lenzner and Johnson, "Seeing Things as They Really Are," 127.
46. Ibid.
47. Hawkins and Battin, *The Mirage of Continuity*, 11, 12.
48. Katz, "Competitive Strategies for Higher Education in the Information Age," 48.
49. National Research Council, *Preparing for the Revolution*, 2.
50. Keller, *Academic Strategy*, 19.
51. Ibid.
52. Morrison, *Using Futures Research in College and University Planning*, 1.

53. Hughes, "A Comparison of Perceptions of Campus Priorities," 140.
54. Breivik and Gee, *Higher Education in the Internet Age,* xi.
55. Lewis, "A Strategy for Academic Libraries in the First Quarter of the 21st Century," 418.
56. Bogart, ed., *The Bowker Annual,* 48th ed., 426.
57. OCLC Online Computer Library Center, *Libraries: How They Stack Up,* 3.
58. Ibid., 5.
59. Bogart, ed., *The Bowker Annual,* 48th ed., 443.
60. Wallman, "Introduction: Contemporary Futures," 3.
61. Crawford and Gorman, *Future Libraries: Dreams, Madness & Reality*, 3.
62. Bennett, *Libraries Designed for Learning,* 3.
63. Ibid.
64. Ibid., 4.
65. Ibid.
66. Bennett, "Libraries and Learning: A History of Paradigm Change," 194.
67. Bennett, "The Choice for Learning," passim.
68. Bennett, "Libraries Designed for Learning," 5–6.
69. Bennett, "Righting the Balance," 18.
70. O'Connor and Bennett, "The Power of Place in Learning," 3.
71. Bennett, "First Questions for Designing Higher Education Learning Spaces," 14.
72. Bennett, "Campus Cultures Fostering Information Literacy," 148.
73. Gleick, *Faster: The Acceleration of Just About Everything,* 9.
74. Bertman, *Hyperculture: The Cost of Human Speed,* 1.
75. Naughton, *A Brief History of the Future: From Radio Days to Internet Years in a Lifetime.*
76. Maloney et al., "Future Leaders' Views on Organizational Culture," 322.
77. Baines, "Management Forecasting," 6.
78. Keller, *Academic Strategy: The Management Revolution in American Higher Education,* 67.
79. Nicole, "Preface," iv.
80. Bryson, *Strategic Planning for Public and Nonprofit Organizations,* 158.
81. Bolling, The Art of Forecasting, 2.
82. Baines, "Management Forecasting," 6.
83. Allain, *Futuristics and Education,* 11, 13; Martino, "Forecasting and Its Impact on Policymaking," 111.

CHAPTER FOUR

Research Methodology and Decision Maker Distinctives

Introduction

By way of review, the decision making model applied to this research portrays organizational decision making as an environment where

> [O]rder emerges from the random interaction of problems, solutions, choice situations, and participants, rather than from intentions, plans, and consistent decisions. Timing and participation can shape outcomes. Managers' decisions can be influenced by people with whom they happen to be meeting, pressure to address problems that are thrust suddenly into the spotlight, windows of opportunity that can be linked with an existing problem and the existence of a pet solution.[1]

In metaphorical terms, multiple—*largely independent*—"streams" flow through an organization: decision making **participants, problems** needing **solutions,** solutions looking for problems, and **windows of opportunity** (choice situations) that bring the streams together (coupling) to make decisions possible. The decision-effects of the often serendipitous interaction of these streams can neither be thoroughly identified in advance, nor fully controlled at any point. Though hindsight can make some sense of how a decision took place, the variables in each stream change with each iteration and the new mix is no more predictable or controllable than the former mix.

How did library directors and other key decision making participants describe decision making—including the use of technology forecasts—during the construction of new academic libraries? Did their descriptions comport with the idea of serendipitous interactions of independent streams? This was answered through an analysis of transcripts from tape recorded interviews. More than 300 pages of interview transcripts were read and analyzed using categories derived from the decision making research of Cohen et al.[2] and Kingdon.[3]

Twenty participants from five colleges and universities in five different states spanning three time zones were interviewed. Participants were involved in the decision making process for building a new academic library at institutions with enrollments from 1,100 to 24,000. Project costs ranged from only $1,000,000—for a specialized graduate school library on a large state university campus—to $42,000,000 for a small private college with 1,600 students.

A wide variety of participants were interviewed based on cohorts named by each library director: architects, vice presidents, physical plant/building and grounds managers, professional library staff, a director of campus planning, a consultant, and an academic dean.[4] Furthermore, this variety is amply expanded by the additional decision making participants mentioned during the interviews: students, boards of trustees, state agencies, chancellors, faculty, donors, alumni, and even library users from the local community.

While each of these individuals is a natural candidate for a decision making role during the construction of an academic library, one position is notable for its *absence* from the list. None of the five directors named a vice president for academics or provost for inclusion in the decision making cohort and only one of the twenty participants named a provost among those who were perceived to be significantly influential during the library construction process.

The findings of this research support the descriptive rigor of the decision making model of Cohen et al., sometimes in surprising ways. Decision making was *often* a matter of the sorting and resorting of variables *in the present* instead of rationally articulated plans based on firm visions of the future. Indeed, instead of stable decision makers working in the midst of fluid circumstances, we find that these *decision makers are also remarkably fluid*. This phenomenon will be described next, under the findings related to the participant stream.

The Participant Stream

The participant stream is populated by all those individuals—or groups of individuals—who influence the decision making process and hence the change process.⁵ A prominent feature of decision making participants emerged from this research, a phenomena I have dubbed **Asymmetric Influence.** The asymmetric influence among decision making participants undercuts many of the assumptions of the political decision making model.

To paraphrase March⁶—substituting the word "influence" for "power"—influence is domain specific: A person influential in one domain is not necessarily influential in another. There is not a single index of influence for an individual decision maker, but different influences for different decision arenas.

In the context of this study, one domain of influence is the domain of *other* decision makers. Different decision makers are influenced differently by other decision makers, *even in the same setting.* Decision maker "A" and decision maker "B" are influenced in different ways and to different degrees by decision maker "C" and so on. The more participants there are in the decision making process, the more inscrutable the calculus and the more asymmetric the influence.

For this research, each library director was asked: "Which individuals stand out in your memory as having been most influential in the decision making process?" During the interviews, each of those individuals was asked the same question. The striking lack of symmetry in the responses is illustrated in Table 1. In the table, each numbered column represents a participant in the study. A shaded square shows who that participant named in answer to the interview question above. A shaded square with a number in it indicates that a single participant named that number of individuals holding the same position, e.g. participant number one at site B named two different individuals at the physical plant. The bottom row, percent overlap, gives the percentage of shaded squares that were duplicated in the replies at each site.

Statistical conclusions cannot be drawn from this table, but it does reveal a broad and significant pattern. Even allowing for the likelihood that all participants would affirm the *importance* of every source of influence in the leftmost column, the asymmetric pattern of perceived *level* of influence is notable. The low overlap at each site accentuates the asymmetry.

Table 1 also illustrates how actual decision making can be in dissonance with intuitive assumptions as well as expectations implied by other decision making models. Note, for instance, the remarkably low influence of both provosts and heads of IT.

Table 1: Asymmetric Influence																				
	Site A				Site B			Site C					Site D				Site E			
	1	2	3	4	1	2	3	1	2	3	4	5	1	2	3	4	1	2	3	4
ad hoc committee																				
alumni																				
architects																				
consultant																				
donor																				
faculty																				
head of IT																				
library director																				
librarians, other						2	2													
library staff							2													
nobody																				
physical plant					2		2													
president																				
provost																				
school dean																				
single administrator																				
staff																				
students																				
vp business																				
percent overlap				23			44					22				41				22

Asymmetric influence may be one of the systemic effects of "fluid participation." Cohen et al. observed that "participants vary in the amount of time and effort they devote to different domains; involvement varies from one time to another… audiences and decision makers for any particular kind of choice change capriciously."[7] As documented next, the data for this research offer strong support for the presence of fluid participation in the participant stream.

What traits characterized those who influenced the decision making process? Table 2 shows the pattern of traits that surfaced when the transcripts were read with this question in mind. The primary characteristic of participants was their fluid participation in the decision making process.

	Table 2: The Participant Stream				
65	fluid participation	22	emotions	12	limited knowledge
31	attention pattern	19	multiple interest groups	10	personalities
27	agendas	17	entrepreneurship	9	process comprehension
26	decision styles	14	organizational placement		

Fluid participation—appearing more than twice as many times as any other characteristic—is a keystone feature of the decision research of Cohen et al., accounting for a significant portion of the temporal sorting and resorting crucial to the descriptive credibility of the model.[8] Documentation for all of the categories in Table 2 are provided in the following paragraphs.

Fluid Participation

When a library director was asked "Was the membership of the decision making cohort the same throughout the process?" her answer was "It came and it went. It coalesced and it didn't coalesce…People came into the group and went out of the group…" After affirming that "there were transitions all about, administration, faculty and library staff, and about the same time" another participant at this site said "It just sort of happened. It was a change."

The director at a second site described significant changes on the building committee over the course of the project. When asked "Did the building committee ever try to go back and revisit things that previously composed committees had already settled?" she answered—with some hyperbole—"Every five minutes."

A third site experienced an almost unsettling amount of fluid participation. The institution went through an administrative reorganization and one participant remembered "a period of time where you're waiting to find out who the new person is and the old person's sort of like, 'I'm not going to those meetings anymore.'" Another participant mentioned a midstream change at the university. They "changed architects from the programming planning stage into the schematic design" and another added "We not only changed architects, we switched engineers. They didn't necessarily pick up on the nuances." A librarian also noted that "we had a lot of turnover among the librarians during that time period. It was a pretty dizzying few years." At this site there "was a lot of changing going on" with participant transitions at "just about every level."

Attention Pattern

The effects of the construction project on participant attention pattern varied, with the most distraction experienced by library directors and staff. Whereas the project was just the next thing on the list for some architects, consultants, and even business vice-presidents, it was a massive add-on for librarians. As put by one library director:

> This project was above and beyond my normal duties. In addition to maintaining my regular schedule, and teaching classes, and serving on committees and attending various meetings…I had, for two years, the building. I added an additional 40% to my regular eight hour a day workload, so I spent countless hours and weekends doing nothing but this project…I found that I had to be able to focus on one thing and be able to change gears immediately when problems with the new building came up. I was expected—by the administration and others—to just add this to everything else.

When asked "Did you struggle to keep your other responsibilities in balance?" a librarian at another site replied "I just didn't do them."

Hence, decision making in other arenas was affected to a significant degree. Especially with regard to the library directors, their ability to engage institution level decision making was altered by the library construction project. They became fluid participants by "floating" out of other decision arenas on campus, affecting the shifting stream combinations in *those* settings. The quotes in Table 3, come from all five sites.

Agendas

Participant perception of agendas held by others ranged from "I don't really think there were any pre-existing agendas" at one site to "there were [so many] agendas that you could beat them with a stick" at another site. The balance of comments were somewhere between these two extremes.

Table 3: Project Effects on Participant Attention Pattern
"[M]any of us were doing two jobs the whole time… Some things were not done as well as they should have been."
"[I]t certainly did draw me away from other responsibilities."
"It was extremely time-consuming…. I can't give you a percentage, but there was a five-year period of time that was kind of a blur….I think everybody was working at 110%….It's not something that I want to do again. It literally is very consuming."
"[T]hings came at us so fast and furious…We just didn't have time…. At times it was just crazy. At times, it was just really, really difficult."
"All that I can tell you is that as you get near the end of the project, and everybody is worn out, the compromises become a lot easier… You're getting down near the end and everybody wants to finish."
"The building committee could have been a full time job in and of itself."
"Everybody…worked like dogs."

When asked about pre-existing agendas brought to the decision making process during construction, one library director stated that "there was this undercurrent of agenda" coming out of the office of the vice president for business:

> The main pre-existing agenda that I think was there in the VP for business was that [the new library] was going to be a floating party barge for the board of trustees and other events that we wanted to give…I was called to the vice president's office of business and he said I want you to draw up the rules and how much we are going to charge when we rent the library out for things like wedding receptions.

At another site, the president brought his own agenda to the process:

> The president was hoping that we would create a boardroom over here. Also, he had hoped that we

might have a big theater in this building…So what was happening in many cases was the president really wanted a place for students to watch a movie and a place for the board to be.

Finally, whereas pre-existing agendas may be described as an "undercurrent"—as in the first illustration above—they may also work as a "hidden current." The following observation was made by one of the architects:

> The college claimed that they were dedicated to a fully transparent decision-making process, meaning [the] administration has said you guys are going to get a new building and the new user and a broad campus constituency will be included in the planning process. But the truth was, behind the scenes, there was one strong headed administrator who believed he had the taste police on his side.…he did kind of force a certain amount of falseness into the presentation. For instance, we were scheduled to give a design meeting one week and then he would decide a week before that I would have a private sit-down with him to preview what we were going to show to make sure he was going to like it.…It did create crazy tension as you can imagine. It created an atmosphere of distrust that the architects had to bear.

Decision Styles

Behavior consistent with the other four decision making models—rational, bureaucratic, political, and collegial—appeared throughout the interviews. But not a single participant described decision making related to library construction as exclusively one or the other. Some emphasized good faith efforts at collegiality and others bemoaned bureaucratic or political confusion. This lends support to the proposition that these models fall short as descriptive representations of what actually occurs in organizational decision making.

The amalgam of decision styles at single sites further illustrates the descriptive utility of decision research by Cohen et al. For instance, at one site where a new president was "moving into a much more transparent governance process," a participant used the phrase "completely participatory" in reference to the design process during library construction. But another participant at the same site revealed some tension between time constraints and collegial process:

> You can run into problems if the time that it takes to go through the process is not available or not permitted. You know it's—if you're hearing from the top we want it collaborative, but you have to do it in three months.

A third participant at this site stated: "There were a lot of politics in this project" and the fourth talked about a particularly influential vice president, saying tactfully that "collegiality was not his forte."

At another site one participant stated that the extent of collaboration—the high level of collegiality—was at times "frustrating" for him:

> [W]e might have not only a long discussion, but maybe multiple, multiple discussions. We would revisit something over and over again that in terms of the larger project, wasn't that significant an issue. Sometimes, we seemed to get into deliberative mode and couldn't pull the trigger…I tend to want to pull the trigger and move on. And other people, just by their nature, want to explore every nook and cranny. So sanity is sometimes somewhere in between.

This participant's decision style did not match the institutional decision style. The same is evident, but in reverse, in these comments from a different site:

> Well, [the library director] did probably ninety percent of the planning on the building and he is very hands-on…I think my style is a little more collaborative, a little more consensus-oriented than [the library director's] style is.…So, I probably would have been a little more collaborative, inviting a little more input into the design and spaces. Like I say, as it turned out, he has

very good taste and very good judgment and it turned out okay. There were a few things that didn't work out too well that I think were directly attributable to him not getting more input.

Finally, the experience of fluid participation affected the mix of decision styles in the middle of one construction project. There was a transition in a dean's position. When asked how this affected decision making the participant said:

Well, I think [dean A] delegates more. He delegates more. [Dean B] is very hands-on and retains more control so more things had to be run by the dean in that phase with [dean B]. There was less of someone feeling like they could make a decision without his input.

Emotions

Participants from every site touched upon the presence of strong emotions associated with the building project. Comments included interpersonal conflict—"There were some unpleasant conversations…a lot of sniping and bickering going on"—as well as personal stress: "The last two years of the building process were very painful to me.…I'm glad the building's built. I'm thrilled. And some day I'll get over it." The only library director to decline participation in this research did so because of the emotional pain that remained. During our brief phone conversation when I called to recruit him for an interview, he quietly said: "Too much turmoil would be brought back to the surface which I would rather put to rest." For one "It caused some sleepless nights" and for another "I lost a significant amount of weight over this project." One participant admitted that as she read some files in preparation for our interview she had the thought "oh this is bringing back a nightmare." After saying that the building project had been "very time-consuming and stressful" a participant remembered "we went to two library projects where the library directors were divorced during a building project" for reasons associated with work stress. A participant at still another site said "I cannot tell you how many of us had trooped to the doctor to get something to help us sleep." One library director was especially vivid in her description:

I'm telling you, going into this I was very nervous. I was scared about the whole thing…could I handle it and how many major mistakes would I make…it demanded an enormous amount of time and thought and waking up in the middle of the night and dreaming about it and all of that, and being desperately afraid…I did not take a vacation for two-and-a-half years and I didn't realize how stretched I was. And my secretary came to me one day and said "you know you're getting a bit tense." And I'm pretty easy going and I don't yell and scream at people, but I could tell that I was getting a slight personality change. And so I went to the doctor, and I sat down and I said to him "Help me! Somebody please help me!" And he said, "I think you need a cocktail of anti-stress medication to get you through the next six months."

Multiple Interest Groups

One of the library directors said "I was always surprised at the amount of ownership every constituency had.…Everybody had an opinion on everything all the time." It was a physical plant director, however, who gave the most descriptive survey of multiple interest groups:

Of course, the library people, they're looking for a building that's going to suit their needs and be attractive, clean, and healthy. Mechanically, some of the guys from the building and grounds department are on that committee, they were looking at this equipment, "am I going to maintain it?", I want something that's accessible. Don't put the filters up on the ceiling where I can't reach it. Keep them down where everything is accessible. Our building officials are interested in sprinkler systems and in fire detection and fire alarm systems. Our computer people are interested in where they are going to get their hook-ups and where are they going to have their wireless receivers. The architect is shooting for the design that he wants. He wants this building to be the showplace.

Additional interest groups mentioned in the interviews included security departments, students, administrators, trustees, donors, faculty, and state government.

Entrepreneurship

In the decision making model of Cohen et al. and Kingdon, entrepreneurs are active change agents who lay claim to a hearing through expertise, position, connections, or negotiating skill. Entrepreneurs are located throughout the organization and they soften up the system over time by persistently floating and refining proposals framed as solutions. These change agents remain alert for favorable timing in which they can claim that their proposal is a solution to a pressing problem. Entrepreneurs frame and define problems in terms of pet solutions. They "lie in wait for a window to open. In the process of leaping at their opportunity, they play a central role in coupling the streams at the window."[9] Thus, although the three decision making streams—participants, problems, and solutions—are complex, unpredictable, and uncontrollable, entrepreneurial participants that construe a relationship that allows a decision to occur. It is somewhat artificial, therefore, to discuss entrepreneurs separately from coupling. But seeing entrepreneurs and coupling as discreet phenomena is necessary for seeing them in tandem. Coupling is described in a section of its own later in this chapter.

An entrepreneurial library director explained that under "the previous library director" the "library wasn't held in very high esteem by the administration." When she came to campus, she noticed that "the building was a major hindrance to students' acceptance of the library on campus" so she started a fund raising group: "I knew our top priority had to be planning for additional library space." In addition to the fund raising group, she started a second group to work symbiotically with the first:

> We put together a task force, and we included a man who was an architect and a member of our library fund-raising board called the Library Advisory Board, as well as faculty and campus planners and other appropriate people. As we went through an analysis of our space utilization and our space needs, and were ready to do a final report, the architect suggested that we really needed a whole new building. And I thought,

> "Well, that's a big idea; let's go with that!" So that was
> one of our ideas. So *we had laid the groundwork....We
> had a proposal in the hopper* [italics added].

This director softened up the system, she remained alert for favorable timing, and she leapt at the point of opportunity.

At another site, entrepreneurs from the library and administration softened up the system *over time* this way:

> I think one of the things that also was *forward-thinking*
> [italics added] on the college's part, was that we knew
> we needed a library and there was a potential for a gift.
> We started the master plan process prior to this gift
> so we were actually *in the process* [italics added] where
> this building would go *when* [italics added] the gift
> materialized.

The discipline of lying in wait—working for when a potential gift might materialize—is also evident. At this site, however, two other major academic buildings were competing for dominance on the agenda. A non-library administrator on campus said that two factors finally combined in favor of the library. First a "history of documentation" provided by the library director and second "the force of an accreditor." The library director used data over time in an entrepreneurial fashion—documenting a pressing problem and proposing a particular solution—and the accreditor created a focusing event that put the library first in line when the financial gift was received.

One library director's entrepreneurial virtue of persistence became evident as she described how difficult it was

> to keep the project alive when the state was pulling the
> money. It was very hard....I went around and spoke to
> our donors and told them we are going to get it done
> and they just had to stay with us. And I just never gave
> up. It wasn't an option. There were some faculty who
> would have given up a time or two....And I just kept
> pushing....You just have to be prepared to push hard,
> *constantly and for a long time* [italics added]. There is

a new geology building on our campus that opened while I was dean. They'd been after a new building for thirty years.

Whereas entrepreneurial initiative alone guarantees nothing, entrepreneurs are essential to coupling. As indicated in the next quote from the interviews, the absence of entrepreneurial behavior can be a significant factor in the decision making process:

> Even before I came in '87, there had been at least one, possibly two committees looking at the need for a new building. And it just never went anywhere....From my perspective, I think it was the director at that time just wasn't a sufficiently strong advocate for the library. I just don't think he had the influence that was necessary.

The entrepreneurial qualities of advocacy (persistently floating proposals) and influence (laying claim to a hearing)—being absent—reduced the likelihood of coupling in favor of the library.

Organizational Placement
The organizational placement of an individual can affect the influence that person is able to wield in a decision making context. The "chain of command" is a force to be reckoned with: "The people who were working on a daily basis together had enough sense to realize when we needed to go higher up the chain of command and ask certain questions and when we could make decisions without asking." Even more to the point from another site:

> In the big view, only the board of trustees has the right to actually make the decision. On a slightly lower level, higher administration, the president and provost, make decisions. The rest of the folks, no matter how much time we all put into it, it's all in the matter of recommendations.

At one site, an institutional reorganization affected the ability of the library to get the attention it needed to convince the university of the need for a new building. In the words of the library director, "It really made a difference…We were pretty far down the totem poll… So we're up front now."

The power of the "chain of command" and the "totem pole" is a core tenet of the political model of decision making. But how this actually works can be easily oversimplified. Influence is asymmetric and power is domain specific:

> A person powerful in one domain is not necessarily powerful in another. There is not a single index of power for an individual decision maker, but different powers for different decision arenas. The domain specificity of power is observed not only in government but also in business firms, families, and churches.[10]

Hence, the distribution of power and how it manifests is neither static, nor quantifiable, nor predictable. Furthermore, different people occupying the same position on the totem may possess different levels of influence due to a host of other variables. For instance, one dean is "powerful" and his successor is "weak." Organizational placement *alone* is not always a predictor of influence or power.

Limited Knowledge

Herbert A. Simon—a Nobel Prize winner in economics—cautioned that "fascination with the pure theory of rational choice has sometimes distracted attention from the problems of decision makers who possess modest calculating powers in the face of a world of enormous complexity."[11] One of the participants seemed to be quoting Simon: "I think you have to understand that it's an enormously complicated process. The level of detail that you might be called upon to engage in is phenomenal."

In addition to the effects of enormous complexity, decisions are also influenced by "selective perception" and "changes in context."[12] Thus, each decision making participant is plagued by 1) limited knowledge; 2) the perception of others regarding the extent of their knowledge; 3) their own perception of the extent of the knowledge of others.

The consultant who was interviewed for this research illustrated the idea of a "knowledge gap" among decision makers:

> I see my role as pretty much a facilitator. What I end up being and doing on these projects, is kind of "fitting." I sit in a gap between the architects and the client. And the reason they ask people like me to work on these things is because there's a kind of knowledge-gap. Most librarians, if they build one building in their lifetimes, it's a lot. And I've done 350. They just don't know. They know a lot about their library. But they're not quite sure, "is this the way we should go?" And I don't quite trust the architects. And the architects don't really know that much about library operations. They know about library buildings, bricks and mortar. But they don't know how things work inside. And so they have to keep being reminded, "Sure it would look great but it won't work."

A director commented that "the most frustrating part was the degree to which members of the internal community could stay un-informed and yet throw rocks from any particular place" and at more than one site there was pressure based on the notion that libraries had already been replaced by the internet. A participant quoted others as saying: "Oh, what do we need a new library for? Everything's electronic." Others recalled statements from individuals such as "print won't last any time." Additional participants remembered similar opinions expressed by others: "One of my first recollections of [the vice president for busi-ness] in one of those meetings was, pushing on the 'what do we really even need a library for anymore?'" and "there was some controversy about building a new library. There were people who thought, 'why bother? The one we have now is good enough. And, besides everything is online'" and "If students can do all their research from their dorm room or sitting outside on a lawn somewhere, do you need a library?"

Finally, a participant from an architectural firm spoke with unusual candor. He said that at the beginning of the project his role was just to sit and listen. I asked him what sorts of things he said to himself while he listened. His response: "Sometimes, how can anybody be so stupid?"

Personalities
The effect of personality traits can be perceived in both favorable and unfavorable light in relation to decision making. At one site, a partici-

pant recalled that "It was incredibly difficult while it was occurring but it was amazingly easy compared to some of the stories I've heard.…I account for it with the personalities, to an extent." At a different site, however, personality was blamed for an unpleasant level of discord: "there were some personality things going on there involving librarians and faculty." One participant believed that decision making styles were "personality driven" and another believed that the success of the whole process can rise or fall "depending upon many different things—on personalities, on the nature and homogeneity of your institution, on funding." At one school a certain design feature was rejected because "organizationally, with some very strong personalities, we were never going to do that" and at another site a participant lamented "I don't know about other places but to a big extent there's a lot of personality driven decision making that goes on here."

Process Comprehension[13]

Cohen et al. observed that an organization's "own processes are not understood by its members"[14] and Kingdon later added that "members have only fragmentary and rudimentary understandings of…how their jobs fit into a more general picture of the organization."[15] Contrary to expectations, however, interview participants generally affirmed a reasonable comfort level with their understanding of organizational decision making processes—and how these processes worked—during the library construction project. One participant, though, did describe a different experience. He stated that among most college faculties in his region of the country

> [Y]ou're going to end up with a bunch of very liberal, capital "L", thinkers. Everyone is equal, we're all the same. It's this utopia. And then you have the capital letter "A" administrators who think very differently, that you guys can go do what you want. Go ahead and be a committee but in the end, it's going to be my decision. There were two very different understandings of the structures and the protocols. The reality was somewhere in the middle.

Nevertheless, no apparent pattern emerged to support a broad presence of confusion over process. Participants were asked questions directly related to process comprehension and so the absence of a pattern expected from the decision research of Cohen et al. is quizzical.

An explanation for this might be found in Kingdon's observations related to "focusing events." Kingdon introduced the idea of a "focusing event" to refer to an attention getting "crisis or disaster that comes along…a powerful symbol that catches on, or the personal experience of a policy maker."[16] If the idea of a focusing event is nuanced to refer to any critical event that focuses the attention of decision makers then perhaps it can contribute to an understanding of why low process comprehension was not prominent during the construction of libraries. The unique, once in a lifetime experience of building an academic library may have been a focusing event for participants. At least for the duration of the project, process comprehension seems to have taken on a level of perhaps atypical clarity.

Conclusion

Decision makers—members of the "participant stream"—were true exemplars of participants within the decision making model of Cohen et al. Instead of stable decision makers working in the midst of fluid circumstances, we find that these *decision makers are also remarkably fluid and the influence they have upon one another is completely asymmetric.* Decision makers with preferences and priorities prone to fluctuate interact with shifting situations and events with stop-and-go time and attention. These characteristics contributed to decision making that was *often* a matter of the sorting and resorting of variables *in the present* instead of rationally articulated plans based on firm visions of the future. The often serendipitous interaction of variables *within* the participant stream amplifies serendipity in the interaction of the participant stream with the problem and solution streams.

Notes

1. Barry, Cramton, and Carroll, "Navigating the Garbage Can," 27.
2. Cohen, March, and Olsen, "A Garbage Can Model of Organizational Choice."
3. Kingdon, *Agendas, Alternatives, and Public Policies.*
4. More than 300 pages of transcripts containing over 130,000 words were produced. As with the abstracts used to answer research question one, all of the transcripts were imported into NVIVO7, a software program used for research involving qualitative text analysis. Each transcript was read and analyzed using categories derived from the decision making research of Cohen et al. (1972) and Kingdon (1995): participants, problems, solutions, and coupling. A fifth broad category,

forecast comments, was included to record content related to the three primary forecast topics discovered in the literature in the years leading up to 2008: impact of technology on collections, the impact of technology on services, and library technology *per se*.

5. This stream is analogous to Kingdon's political stream, a stream composed of social phenomena on a macro level such as "national mood," "election results," and "interest group pressure" (Kingdon, "Agendas, Alternatives, and Public Policies," 87). Kingdon's political stream is nuanced toward the *collective* force of individuals who influence the decision making process, whereas the emphasis of this study is on the perspectives of *individual* decision makers.

6. March, *A Primer on Decision Making: How Decisions Happen*, 143.

7. Cohen, March, and Olsen, "A Garbage Can Model of Organizational Choice," 1.

8. Cohen, March, and Olsen, "A Garbage Can Model of Organizational Choice."

9. Kingdon, *Agendas, Alternatives, and Public Policies*, 181.

10. March, *A Primer on Decision Making: How Decisions Happen*, 143.

11. Simon, "Administrative Decision Making," 33.

12. Plous, *The Psychology of Judgment and Decision Making*, 13.

13. The phrase "process comprehension" was chosen as a replacement for the phrase "unclear technology," an idea contained in the first expositions of the garbage can model. Writing in 1972, Cohen et al. meant technology in the sense of administrative mechanisms, not merely computer based tools.

14. Cohen, March, and Olsen, "A Garbage Can Model of Organizational Choice," 1.

15. Kingdon, *Agendas, Alternatives, and Public Policies*, 84.

16. Ibid., 94, 95.

CHAPTER FIVE

Problems Need Solutions and Solutions Need Problems

Introduction

As noted in chapter 4, the decision making model applied to this research portrays multiple—*largely independent*—"streams" that flow through an organization: decision making **participants, problems** needing solutions, **solutions** looking for problems, and **windows of opportunity** (choice situations) that bring the streams together (coupling) to make decisions possible. Individual decision making participants, as well as groups of participants, see the relationships amongst themselves in unique—even idiosyncratic—ways. Their attention and participation floats in and out of decision making settings, creating an ebb and flow to their influence. This affects the kind and level of influence they exert on decision making as well as the way they see the problems and solutions that flow through the process.

The Problem Stream

For the purposes of this research, a problem was defined as something that someone wants to change. Items can appear in the problem stream as objective problems (e.g. the basement is infested with mold) or simply because they prop up someone's pet "solution." A furniture salesman can "discover" many problems that his furniture happens to solve. Problems have features that affect the way they appear to decision makers and the same set of problems can appear differently to different decision makers, even within the same context. Eventually, "one set of problems rather than another comes to occupy officials' attention"[1] but this is far from a straightforward or transparent process. The true provenance of a problem chosen for solution can be inextricable.

Within the transcripts, an item in the problem stream was identified by answering the question: What contributed to the rise or fall of a problem on the agenda? Table 4 illustrates the pattern of variables in the problem stream.

Table 4: The Problem Stream			
42	physical limitations	8	external standards
12	focusing events	6	feedback
11	benchmark incongruence	5	indicators
9	aesthetics	4	symbolic value
9	value incongruence	3	financial factors

Coherent with the context of building projects, "physical limitations" stands out as the most commonly expressed concern among participants.

Physical Limitations

Nearly half of all the comments for the problem stream related to physical limitations. Participants in 16 of the 20 interviews mentioned such things as decrepit facilities and space issues for students, staff and collections. The following comments are representative of the whole:

> There was just an extreme space shortage. It was very technologically unfriendly. I used to say it was the state of the art of the Eisenhower administration. What this meant was that if you wanted to run a new computer cable, the guy with the concrete drill had to come over, things like that…It was extremely hard to adapt, especially because we were choking on lack of space. The floors were sagging because of the load on them, books were stored in the basement where there [was] just supposed to be spiders. It was a very confining situation…

One kind of space issue, not related to the amount of space but the arrangement of space, was humorously described by a reference librarian:

> In the old building, our offices were essentially glass cubicles in the middle of the floor, [in the middle of] the collection. The idea was that you would put these science librarians in with the science collections and users could find us… The downside of it was that we

were sitting in a glass cubicle out in the middle of the floor trying to get our work done…I can remember sitting on the floor in my office so that my head would not be above the glass line. I had to finish doing what I was doing. There was really no way to work. We had become a little obsessed with having private offices [in the new building].

Focusing Events

A focusing event is a crisis or other attention arresting event that brings a perceived problem to the fore and shapes decision making.[2] Interview comments describe focusing events that contributed to decisions to build libraries as well as focusing events that occurred during the construction projects. The most common focusing event prior to construction had to do with unfavorable accreditation reviews: "our accreditation agency just rained all over us. [When the accreditation agency] says 'you know, there's an accreditation issue here' it wakes people up; it gets their attention." At the same site a different participant added that the accreditor threatened to put the school on provisional status and that "this is what got the legislature's attention." At another site, after noting that the accrediting agency "hit the old building pretty hard" the participant noted "we then got a new president who paid attention."

A different kind of focusing event, caused by a mold infestation, was experienced at one site. There, the library building "had major air handling problems." As described by the participant,

> [W]e had gone through one summer with a huge mold infestation on one floor. They had to come in and peel up the floor and actually clean every single book. Personally, I was one of the people that had to be relocated because the mold really got to me. And a couple of other people had triggered terrible asthma attacks… we had some summer students who came to work for a week and their doctors were like, you've got to quit. That happened one summer and then the following summer we had a slight infestation again and we had to clean mold. They had to replace ductwork in the library and we couldn't keep the humidity under control.

Benchmark Incongruence

A benchmark is a standard of measure. In the problem stream, "benchmark incongruence" is a condition where some accepted standard of measure is not being met. As illustrated in the following quote, benchmarks can be set by looking at peer institutions:

> the college has pretty lofty aspirations [in terms of] who we like to look at as our "aspirant peers"… our print collection holds up pretty well in comparison to other public institutions in [the state]. [But] if we looked at our print collection compared to our aspirant peers, we were in pretty sorry shape. So then… knowing that if we wanted to have a collection that we could point to [as] being something like our aspirations, then we would have to account for better collection development [in the new building].

Aesthetics

Participants from four of the five sites described aesthetic problems in the following ways: there was a "lack of welcoming space;" the building looked "like an early bomb shelter with ugly green shelves, dingy, dirty;" "It was dark and gloomy. You really didn't want to come there;" "the old building was so dang dark… the lighting in the old building was poor… in the old building you would have to crawl around on your hands and knees to try to read the call numbers on the bottom shelf;" "it was turning into a kind of pit… and it just started looking uglier and uglier the longer we were there."

Value Incongruence

A value is something held to be of worth. In the problem stream, "value incongruence" is a condition where something of worth is inadequate or absent. Incongruence related to the value of stack browsing is evident in this comment:

> [O]ur stacks went all the way to the ceiling and were only 28 inches apart. They were filled with books and—because of the way the light was shielded by the books on the top shelf—you had to take a flashlight to

> go down on the ground floor to actually find anything.
> So needless to say there was very little if any browsing.
> You couldn't do it to any extent, you couldn't do it.

Other participants talked about the value of space for group study, space for bibliographic instruction, and space for adequate offices. In each case, conditions were incongruent with these values. For instance, at one site "we were just literally living in each other's pockets... I couldn't even get out of my office without going through somebody else's."

External Standards

Whereas benchmarks are chosen by the institution, external standards are imposed on the institution. Likewise, the most common problem with external standards had to do with unfavorable accreditation reviews. The combination of a focusing event (a crisis or other attention arresting event that shapes decision making) and a failure to meet external standards added to the potency of this problem within the overall institutional problem stream. At one site yet another matter, one related to legal external standards and steeped in symbolic value, combined with the focusing event of an unfavorable accreditation review: "our old building was not ADA compliant."

Feedback

Feedback is defined as observations made by others that something is wrong, that something needs to change. Feedback can be sought, as in the use of consultants and student surveys, or it can be received through informal comments made by others.

Participants at three of the five sites mentioned the use of consultants. This comment illustrates what consultants for each site in this study typically concluded: "we hired a consultant to come in and look at the building. And he basically said it wouldn't be worth expanding it or renovating it...And it just wasn't going to fit what a library was going to be like, now or in the future or ever."

One library director was very systematic about the use of student surveys as a way to accumulate feedback over time: "I did surveys every other year—I've done them every other year for 15 years—of about 600 of the student body; we have 1100... And what they said to us was it's too hot it's too cold. It's too dark it's uncomfortable. The furniture looks like it came from 1965—which it did because that's when the building was built. We can't study, it's too noisy…"

Statements from two different sites illustrate feedback of a more informal nature: "people didn't like it, they thought it was ugly, the tour guides wouldn't take prospective students in there—I mean you can't blame them" and "the building was a major hindrance to students' acceptance of the library on campus."

Indicators

An "indicator" is a concrete observation that creates a concern. So, for instance, one participant said "we saw declining usage… we had maxed out the building electricity-wise. I couldn't pull enough cables in there to house the number of PCs that we needed… we had three group study rooms and they were constantly in use." At another site, a participant remembered that "it had gotten to the point where the library was sort of the joke. We were so ugly… even in the student newspaper, it was, we were sort of the joke. And people assumed we had nothing." At a third site the library was, for many, "just a place to avoid."

Symbolic Value

The "symbolic value" of something rests in its power to point beyond itself to something perceived as greater than itself. Words, artifacts, and actions all have potential to carry symbolic value. Singing the Star Spangled Banner while waving an American flag illustrates all three. The symbolic value of something in the problem stream is bound with its perceived ability to point beyond itself. The poor condition of the library as a symbol for academic quality campus wide is illustrated by this description:

> [I]n the mid-nineties there was a general discontent that reached a revolting phase among the faculty against the president… And interestingly, a neglect of academics was the faculty's main agenda item. And frankly the library was used like a poster child: "Look at the neglect the library has suffered over the years." So, frankly, when the old president was pretty much forced out and the new president was hired, a

neglect of academics and pointing at the library was a good example. This was put to all of the candidates [for president] and [it was]something that the new president recognized as a legitimate gripe.

Participants at a second site spoke of the library's poor condition as a matter that affected the "prestige" and "respect" of the college.

Financial Factors

Perhaps most problems could be placed in this category since most problem solutions seem to have a financial cost. But not all problems are perceived or described as *primarily* financial in nature. This was not a common problem category but participants at two different sites offered revealing statements about the financial angle of the problem description. If a problem is something that someone wants to change and if cash flow is defined as a problem—and if an inadequate library is seen as a partial cause of less than optimal cash flow—then an inadequate library is a choke point in the cash flow. At one school this was framed in terms of recruitment, a major variable in a school's financial condition:

> The drive for a new building was really an acknowledgement that the old library and its aesthetics were completely dysfunctional for the campus. And I'm sure it had to do with student recruitment. They felt like they had reached a point where their old library was just unacceptable… they said "wow" why don't we build a new building? This is a high enough priority. It's high profile. It's a real recruitment tool so why not invest that in the new library?

At another school it was simply a matter of donor preferences: "they did a survey to see 'where would anybody put their money?'" and the library came to the top.

The Solution Stream

Idealized portrayals of decision making are often framed in terms of focused decision makers who identify problems and opportunities and then choose "solutions" for solving the problems and pursuing the opportunities. Perhaps in a perfectly rational world, there would be a straightforward—almost cause-effect—relationship between problems and solutions. A clean linear sequence could be charted in advance and confirmed in hindsight. But within the world we actually inhabit, the relationship between problems and solutions is at best fragmentary and ambiguous. Furthermore, in actual decision settings "solutions" sometimes come to the table despite or in the absence of clearly articulated problems or opportunities.[3] At times, "solutions" on hand—consider the latest information technology device—are used to fabricate the "problems" and "opportunities" that we "discover" and endorse.

For the purpose of this research a solution was defined as anything that shaped the kind of change that occurred, whether or not the change was anchored in a careful analysis of problems and opportunities. A comment in the solution stream was identified by answering the question: What contributed to the gain or loss of support for a solution?

Table 5: The Solution Stream								
36	influential participant	14	aesthetics	8	pedagogy
30	financial factors	12	external comparisons	7	internal standards
25	flexibility	9	legal constraints	6	trend assumptions
23	value congruence	9	symbolic value	5	external standards
21	expert advice	8	physical factors	4	time constraints
17	user considerations	8	standing policy	2	technical feasibility

Power (influential participants) and money (financial factors) dominate the list. This tempts a reflex in favor of the political model of decision making. But though the influence of these variables was very significant at points, instances of political behavior did not account for all significant instances of decision making. Conspicuously—and disappointingly—low in the comment tally is pedagogy, noted only eight times in 244 solution comments.

Influential Participant
Not surprisingly, influential participants showed up in interviews at all sites. The quotes in Table 6 are drawn from interviews at every site:

Financial Factors
As in the problem stream, financial factors eventually attach to every

Table 6: Statements by Influential Decision Making Participants
"I would say at the time the chancellor that we had was quite in favor of it and understood the importance of having a new library. His wife was also on the library advisory board so we had significant buy-in from the upper administration."
"The influence of the donors on it was—it was—it was not ongoing but it was simply the president made promises to the donors at the beginning."
"[I]n the end, there are some things about the design that were, from my perspective, dictated from above."
"So, in terms of interior décor, we were hostage to our donors' taste."
"And finally one of our donors stepped up, who was one of our alumni, [and said] this building is going to be our library for the next hundred years, let's make it as attractive as possible. The bosses got together… and it's worked out and the building's beautiful."
"The building reflects [the library director]. It is truly her building."
"[I]n all honesty, a number of faculty members hated the dean and wanted to get rid of him. This was his project. The faculty was pretty well able to stop the project and he left about a year and a half later. And then the next dean didn't care one iota about bricks. Then the next dean came in and said 'what a dump.'"

decision variable in the solution stream. In the words of one vice president, a line is drawn and "everything above the line can be afforded and everything below the line cannot." But in some cases, financial factors are more interesting than just drawing a line. The following quote demonstrates how other factors can converge with the financial:

> [W]orking with all of those people to make sure that whether – 'Okay this is a green idea, which you know we want to do.' And, 'Yes, it is actually going to save us energy.'

Here the "green idea"—with symbolic significance—combines as a value (something "we want to do") with the financial "save us energy" (i.e. save us money). The combination of the three strengthened the attractiveness of the "green" solution in decision making.

> At one site, the cost of renovating the old building didn't "make sense" compared with building a new one. They began "reviving the idea" of building a new

building rather than just renovating the existing building, which seemed financially to make a lot more sense. Because, for example, it was going to cost 10 million dollars just to improve the HVAC system in the old building… And putting all that money into that old building didn't seem to make a lot of sense.

At another site, it was actually cheaper to build a new library than to renovate the old one:

> The college intended, as its first try, to renovate and expand the existing facility. We then went through a substantial schematic design phase… Then they costed it out. They didn't like the architect's cost estimate so the college commissioned their own estimators. [Their estimate was only] a hundred thousand dollars off, which is absurd. It was exactly the same. We had a 30 million dollar budget and to have it come off by a hundred thousand dollar difference means that it was exactly the same for all intents and purposes. They then decided, well we can build cheaper than that.

Flexibility

Participants at every interview site emphasized the importance of flexibility as a criterion for weighing solutions. At three sites flexibility was truly a driving factor: "One of our premises was that it would be a really flexible building" and "from day one, we wanted a multi-purpose building that would be extremely adaptable… we tried to make it as flexible and adaptable as possible" and "our main conversations were to remain flexible."

The importance of flexibility was highlighted in terms of future needs. Instead of building a library that reflected a fixed notion of the future, these colleges built libraries that reflected an open ended view of the future: "All the time [we were] thinking, 'If this gives us more flexibility down the road, we'd rather spend it now than spend it later.'"

One participant noted that the old building, having lacked flexibility, did not accommodate unanticipated change over time:

> [W]e really wanted to have as flexible a facility as possible. Because I had worked so long in the old building, I had seen so many modifications to the old building that I was convinced, as were a number of long-timers, that having seen how many changes were being made, we needed to try and stay as flexible as possible with the expectation that something similar is going to happen to this [new] building...

A similar orientation was expressed at another site:

> We knew that we wanted to build a building that would be able to have flexible space so that [as] new ideas emerged in libraries we could alter this space in the new building to try to take advantage of what the next library generation thought what was appropriate for this college.

Other notable comments on flexibility included: "It's a continuous thing of adaptation and we just tried to make spaces that people could change around" and "Everything, even the shelving, as compared to the old building, is flexible and moveable" and "we tried to be as open in the construction as we [could]."

Value Congruence
As noted under value *in*congruence in the problem stream, a value is something held to be of worth. But whereas in the problem stream value incongruence is a condition where something of worth is inadequate or absent, in the solution stream value congruence is a criterion for instilling something of worth. During the interview of a library consultant, he said:

> I think people starting out in building projects [should] think about what the library represents to their institution. What is it about that institution that the library should reflect?" Interviews revealed values related to such things as beauty, comfort, preservation, ecological responsibility and the library as the heart of the cam-

pus. In the words of one participant, "what this new building allowed us to do was to incorporate visions and plans that we couldn't carry out in the old building.

One of the library directors captured the impact that a library building can have on things we value:

> I used a quote from Winston Churchill and I started with the first presentation I ever gave to the board of trustees when I began to draw this up. The quote that I used was 'We shape our buildings and thereafter they shape us.' And that's what I used consistently as a theme all the way through to the talk that I gave when we had the grand opening for the library.

Expert Advice

Comments in this category focused on specific illustrations of when the advice of experts affected the level of support for a solution. Consultants or architects are the subject of all twenty-one instances in this category. These experts were mentioned hundreds of times in the interviews.[4] The contribution of consultants and architects was on the mind of every person interviewed.

In many cases, expert advice by way of hired consultants was cited as a reason for gain in support for a solution. In some cases this was related to the solution for what to do with the old building: "[the consultant from Princeton] said that we wouldn't be able to add onto the existing building in order to meet the needs of the college, that we needed to consider a new building." In other cases consultants affected the gain in support for solutions during construction. Sites hired technology consultants, audiovisual consultants, and planning consultants.

Architects affected support for a solution in much the same way as consultants. As for what to do with the old building, for instance:

> [W]e put together a task force, and we included on that task force a man who was an architect... Well, as we went through an analysis of our space utilization and our space needs, and were ready to do a final report,

the architect suggested that we really needed a whole
new building.

Architects can also influence solution oriented decision making *during* construction: "[T]he lead architects were particularly influen-tial. In many cases, they didn't come to us with, 'What's your biggest dream?' And, then, 'We'll draw what you're dreaming.' They made recommendations." This is an illustration of a point made earlier, that "solutions" sometimes come to the table *despite* or in the *absence* of clearly articulated problems or opportunities.

User Considerations

User considerations—considerations of what students, faculty, and staff needed in the new building—were important at every site. It was described at one site as "the number one criterion" and at another site as "the most important thing." The range of user considerations includes a comprehensive philosophy of building location in relation to the rest of the campus, to one factor such as group study areas.

The concern for user considerations on a grand scale is evident in these remarks from a vice president:

The new building was constructed literally in the center of the campus. It was really at a point where, by design, there was a lot of traffic coming from every direction focusing on that building. This was of course was one of our goals, to increase faculty, staff, and student interaction. We knew we wanted some social places so we built a Star-bucks lounge on the main level. We knew that we wanted academic spaces, seminar rooms, a few classrooms, some computer labs and a whole bunch of study rooms of different sizes.

Collaborative work space in the form of group study areas was men-tioned in multiple contexts. As a criterion in the solution stream, it was even a driving factor at one site: "issues about collaborative work drove not only furniture selection and design but also design for the building."

Aesthetics

In one interview, the aesthetic solution was phrased simply: "we wanted something that was pleasant with lots of natural light." In another case, the arrangement of shelving in the new building had to be addressed after the fact. After the installers arrived with the shelving, a library director noted:

> …it just wasn't right. Aesthetically, there was a problem. And we said we can't do this. What alternatives do we have? Tom was great. He said, "you're right. Aesthetically this is bad. Let's eliminate this row and add this row." And I was like, yeah.

On three of the campuses, the aesthetic solution for exterior appearance was combined with solution by decree. In each case the library was required to duplicate what one architect called the "stylistic vocabulary" of the rest of the campus.

External Comparisons

External comparisons can involve formal benchmarking or they can be as informal as "notes from the field." One director explained benchmarking as a way to resolve decision making conflict:

> So you have those types of conflicts where both people have valid points.…You know a lot of what I will do is benchmarking. I look at what other campuses are doing because sometimes that will answer [important questions].

The quote below was used as an illustration of benchmark incongruence in the problem stream. But after the decision to build a new library, it became an external comparison factor in the solution stream:

> the college has pretty lofty aspirations [in terms of] who we like to look at as our "aspirant peers"… our print collection holds up pretty well in comparison to other public institutions in [the state]. [But] if we looked at our print collection compared to our aspirant peers, we were in pretty sorry shape. So then… knowing that if we wanted to have a collection that we could point to [as] being something like our aspirations, then we would have to account for better collection development [in the new building].

At one college, public libraries were included as part of external comparisons:

> I don't know how many libraries we visited… We went to both public and private academic libraries because some of the new exciting things are going into public libraries…The board chairman flew us to one place in his private jet. We told him we could get used to this.

Another college took advantage of student perspectives: "We tapped the students. We had a student on a team that went and looked at other libraries."

Finally, as illustrated in this advice from a library director, some external comparisons affect decision making by way of negative example: "Visit, visit, visit. Take your other staff members with you. We took hundreds of digital photographs of what we liked and what we didn't like. Often what we didn't like was more important than what we did like."

Sociologists DiMaggio and Powell use the phrase "institutional isomorphism" to describe their observation that "once a set of organizations emerges as a field, a paradox arises: rational actors make their organizations increasingly similar as they try to change them."[5] Higher education and librarianship are examples of "organizational fields" that "provide a context in which individual efforts to deal with uncertainty and constraint often lead, in the aggregate, to homogeneity in structure, culture, and output."[6] In a statement that only the decision research of Cohen et al. can digest, Dimaggio and Powell maintain that "organizations in a structured field… respond to an environment that consists of other organizations responding to their environment, which consists of organizations responding to an environment of organizations' responses."[7]

For instance, in a study of the relationship between investment in information technology and institutional outcomes in higher education, Schwalbe found that "colleges and universities are generally not focusing on pedagogical or productivity related reasons for adopting information technologies."[8] Instead, the focus was on an effort to "emulate peers."[9]

The data for this research shows significant evidence of isomorphic decision making. Evidence for this is found in three categories of the solution stream: expert advice, external comparisons, and external standards. The total of instances for these three is 28. If they were merged into one category—isomorphism—they would represent the third most common phenomenon in the solution stream.

Conclusion

The attention and participation of individual decision makers floats in and out of decision making settings. Decision maker influence ebbs and flows within a dynamic mix of problems and solutions that often have no rational connection. Decision maker interaction with problems and solutions—to continue the stream metaphor—is a constant swirl. How, then, do useful decisions take place? Chapter 6 will explore this question.

Notes

1. Kingdon, *Agendas, Alternatives, and Public Policies*, 87.
2. Ibid., 94, 95.
3. In the words of Cohen et al.,: "a solution is somebody's product" (Cohen, March, and Olsen, "A Garbage Can Model of Organizational Choice," 3).
4. Using the word frequency query in the NVIVO7 software, the terms *architect and architects appear 196 times. Only one other type of person appears more in all interviews, student and students at 236 times. The terms consultant and consultants appear 67 times and so, combined with architect and architects, these experts appear more times than even students: 263 times.*
5. DiMaggio and Powell, "The Iron Cage Revisited," 147.
6. Ibid.
7. Ibid., 149.
8. Schwalbe, *A Study of the Relationship Between Investment in Information Technology and Institutional Outcomes in Higher Education*, 69.
9. Ibid.

CHAPTER SIX

Building the Library: How Decisions Happened

Cohen et al. observed that "choices are made only when the shifting combinations of problems, solutions, and decision makers happen to make action possible."[1] This convergence of problems, solutions, and decision makers (participants) *happens*; it is not rationally *determined*—though it may be rationally discerned. Choices (decisions) are facilitated at the point of convergence by a special class of entrepreneurial participants—active change agents called "policy entrepreneurs" by Kingdon—who discern the convergence and leverage the decision opportunity that the convergence affords. When successful, this phenomenon is called coupling, a term used by Kingdon to describe "a joining of all three streams" that "dramatically enhances the odds that a subject will become firmly fixed on a decision agenda."[2] March uses the phrase "temporal sorting" and adds that "linkages are formed, in part, because of simultaneity."[3]

The elusiveness of this temporal sorting—and convergence leading to stream coupling—is evident in observations made by Jay Lucker, an acclaimed library consultant from the Massachusetts Institute of Technology:

> I've been doing building consulting for a long time. I've worked on about two hundred projects; although I have to say, in nearly thirty years of consulting, I estimate that about 40% of my projects have never resulted in a building. One of the frustrating things about working on buildings is that you do a lot of programming and planning and then the building is never built. You have to accept a certain amount of frustration.[4]

Whereas the phenomenon of non-coupling in relation to library construction does not, of course, appear in this study, coupling followed by *un*coupling succeeded by *re*coupling does appear in interviews from one research site:

> We did our first program plan, on which our subsequent program plan was based, the first was 1986. Then we stopped for 9 or 10 years. In 1996 we started up again and ran full steam until 2002 when we were put on hold by the legislature, and then we started up again in 2004 and redesigned it and built us a building.

The unpredictability of coupling of independent streams is illustrated in the following response from a library director. When asked how he would describe "the convergence of circumstances that allowed the building of the library to come to the top of the agenda" at his college, he replied:

> It's very interesting that you put it that way. And frankly, you're the first person to really hit the nail on the head. Because it really is, or was, a convergence of circumstances. I would be interested to hear how many other places it does come about that way. One was new leadership at the president and provost level. And second was a favorable market because the [college], although we're a public institution, we don't put any state funds—direct state funds, allocated funds—into the capital budget. Every building we build is based on leverage that we float a bond, and we build based on bonds. So the market was right for another state assisted bond. It really was two *independent factors* [italics added].

This participant described the shifting relationship of two *independent factors*—decision makers (president and provost) and the solutions (the bond market). The favorable convergence of these two factors made it possible for an issue in the problem stream, the need for a new library, to join in the convergence resulting in a decision to build. Furthermore the convergence *happened*; it was not *determined*. Both Kingdon and Cohen et al. emphasize the independence of the streams: "Each of the streams has a life of its own, largely unrelated to the others"[5] and "each of the streams can be viewed as independent."[6]

At another site, stream coupling leading to the decision to build a library was described as being the result of the coming together of "multiple advantages." The president was exploring a bond issue at the same time that the administration was doing a classroom space utilization study to justify new classroom construction. At the same time the library director was doing a proposal for a new library and the donor board was promoting the library as a reputation issue:

> [S]o it's very interesting, because at the same time the president of the system was doing this bond issue they were also doing a space utilization study…our space utilization figures for our classrooms looked horrible… So a classroom building was not an option to propose because our local campus administrator, the chancellor, was being told…"You have more classroom space than you need." So that wasn't an option. We were pretty well moving along with the planning process [for a new library], so *I really think it was that combination* [italics added] of being told the space study, rightly or wrongly, found that our classroom space was under-utilized compared to others in the system. We had a proposal in the hopper. Another factor was our donor board; they were very proactive…They definitely kept it on the agenda; kept saying how important it was for not only students and faculty, but for the overall reputation of the university. So, you know, we had kind of *multiple advantages* [italics added].

The shifting combination of problems, solutions, and decision makers sorted out to provide multiple advantages that lead to successful coupling.

Moving to a third site, when asked "how would you describe the convergence of circumstances that allowed this building to rise to the top of the agenda?" the library director replied:

> *Pure unadulterated luck* [italics added]. We had a 1953 building which had pretty much reached its size capacity and was just not adequate…our accrediting agency came in probably about 1988 and they hit the

old building pretty hard as inadequate. We then got a new president who paid attention.…He came in and talked to me right after he arrived and we talked again and I pointed out that the building was not even close to what it should be for a college of this quality…So it tied right in with the [accreditation] report. When the new president got here, we hired a consultant to come in and look at the new building. And he basically said it wouldn't be worth expanding it or renovating it. It was very broken up, 1950's architecture. And it just wasn't going to fit what a library was going to be like. Now or in the future or ever…And soon thereafter, [the president] called a meeting and said, "Everybody come to the auditorium" and he announced the gift which was a legacy from a man who didn't really go to [the college].…He had no heirs basically and of the three trustees of the estate foundation, a couple of them had connection with [the college]…So basically that's how all $35 million plus the interest came to us.

Here the unpredictability and uncontrollability of the streams is emphasized by the sense that things came together through "pure unadulterated luck."

At a fourth site, the "temporal sorting" and "linkages" that "are formed, in part, because of simultaneity" in coupling[7] is evident in the following comments from their library director:

Now keep in mind that there was nothing wrong with the old building that a hand grenade would not have cured.…And our accreditation agency just rained all over us. About the time the accreditor says there's an accreditation issue here it wakes people up, it gets their attention…*Fortuitously* [italics added] we had some people, various people in the building committee just *in the right place at the right time* [italics added]. There were people involved in faculty governance who had the ear of certain administrators…Just *the right fish were in the pond at the right time* [italics added].

At the fifth site, facilities planners hired by the university had identified the library as one of the school's problems in terms of a comprehensive master plan. Building on this, the library director hired a well known library consultant who described the solution in terms of a new library at a new location. The consultant's report along with widespread agreement that the library was no longer adequate convinced the president and board to establish a capital campaign to raise the necessary funds.

At the risk of overdrawing the metaphor, whereas coupling results from the *flowing* together of the process streams—participants, problems, solutions—*microcoupling* is the *swirling* together of elements *within* each stream. Microcoupling appears as an internal phenomenon that affects the rise and fall of specific problems within the problem stream, the waxing and waning of specific solutions within the solution stream, and the ebb and flow of specific participants' influence within the participant stream. Microcoupling shapes what is dominant in each stream at any given time, setting the stage for whether large scale coupling occurs.

A recent illustration of microcoupling is found in decision making on university campuses subsequent to the classroom massacres at Virginia Tech (April 16, 2007) and Northern Illinois University (February 14, 2008). Many campuses have rushed to install rapid emergency alert systems including such capabilities as mass email, phone, and text messaging. Prior to the tragedies at Virginia Tech and Northern Illinois University these capabilities were present in the solution stream on every campus. But in most cases there was no perception of a compelling problem to which the solution could attach. But sudden changes—unplanned and uncontrollable—occurred in the problem stream. Within this single stream, at least two elements converged, or coupled, to force the problem of student safety to the surface of the problem stream: 1) two high profile, high consequence, *focusing events* and 2) the *symbolic value* of breaches in student safety. These breaches were symbolic, not in the sense that they were merely evocative abstractions, but in the sense that the breaches could trigger fears that cascade into other campus contexts—as a symbol points beyond itself, so the breaches pointed beyond themselves. What about the dorms? What about the cafeteria? The subsequent coupling of the three process streams, leading to decisions to install rapid emergency alert systems, was pre-staged by microcoupling in the problem stream. Finally, as with stream coupling, microcoupling *happens*; it is not rationally *determined*—though it may be rationally discerned and leveraged by entrepreneurial participants.

Evidence of microcoupling appeared in problem stream data under external standards. As noted there, the most common *focusing event* prior to construction had to do with unfavorable accreditation reviews. Likewise, the most common problem with external standards had to do with unfavorable accreditation reviews. The combination of a focusing event and a failure to meet external standards added to the potency of this problem within the overall institutional problem stream. At one site yet another matter, one related to legal external standards and steeped in symbolic value, combined with the focusing event of an unfavorable accreditation review: "our old building was not ADA compliant."

Microcoupling also appeared in solution stream data under financial factors. Repeating from that section, the following quote demonstrates how other factors can converge with the financial: "[W]orking with all of those people to make sure that whether – 'Okay this is a green idea, which you know we want to do.' And, 'Yes, it is actually going to save us energy.'" Here the "green idea"—with *symbolic* significance—combines as a *value* (something "we want to do") with the *financial* "save us energy" (i.e. save us money). The combination of the three strengthened the attractiveness of the "green" solution in decision making.

Technology Forecasts and Decision Making

Finally, how did library directors and other key decision making participants describe the use of technology forecasts during the construction of new academic libraries? The short answer to this question is: *with studied agnosticism*. Participants at every site were reluctant to call anything they did "technology forecasting." Paradoxically, however, transcripts are full of data related to decisions about the future, including the role of technology. Furthermore, these decisions still fit the definition of a forecast that I use in this study: "for the purposes of this research, a *technology forecast* is a statement that anticipates, projects, or estimates events or conditions related to possible future effects of a technological innovation." As asserted by Martino, any organization "that can be affected by technological change inevitably engages in forecasting technology whenever there is a decision that allocates resources to particular purposes."[8] So, whereas participants were averse to the *term* "forecasting," they were nonetheless deeply involved in the estimation of conditions related to the future effects of technology. Forecasts were made, but only implicitly.

For the period 1990-2007, the most frequently published forecasts related to technology in libraries focused on the impact of technology on collections, the impact of technology on services, and library technology *per se*.[9] A variety of other topics also appeared in the literature, but at a much lower incidence.

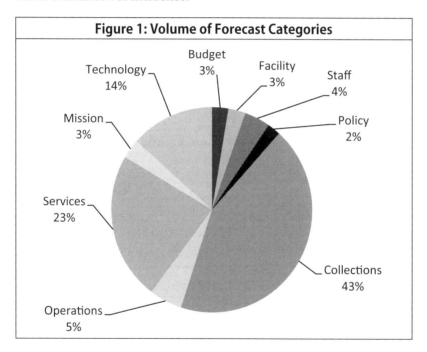

Figure 1: Volume of Forecast Categories

Technology 14%
Budget 3%
Facility 3%
Staff 4%
Policy 2%
Collections 43%
Operations 5%
Services 23%
Mission 3%

Statistical conclusions cannot be drawn from simple counts, but general patterns useful for interpretation do emerge.[10] The most surprising feature of the chart above is the very low representation, at only 3%, of the facilities category. This is remarkable in light of the fact that, after budget considerations, the primary impact of library collection issues—the category with the highest volume (43%)—is space, a facilities matter.

Based on the information above, the interviews for this research explored matters related to assumptions about the interplay between technology forecasts and the future of library collections, library services, and library technology. These topics will be discussed after a look at the pervasive forecast agnosticism expressed throughout the interviews.

Forecast Agnosticism

When one participant was asked "At any point in the process, did anyone introduce a specific technology forecast as the basis for decision making related to the building?" she replied "No. We figured we couldn't tell." In answer to the same question, another participant responded "Can you give me an example? I'm really kind of…" After hearing an example, she said "They're tough. They're really, really tough.…I can do a technology plan for two years but don't ask me to do five. It's very, very difficult." The statements in Table 7, below—each taken from different participants—illustrate the level of uncertainty and ambiguity about technology forecasting.

Table 7: Forecast Agnosticism Among Participants
…none of us knew for sure…
Forecasts. It just seems so perverse to say, my recollection was in terms of technology, the IT folks seemed more cautious than I would have expected.
I don't think we ever had a forecast of "this is exactly what is going to happen or we need to do this because this is the way it's going to be." I'm not quite sure if we still know where we're going.
You know, I don't know if I can point to anything.
No. Nobody asked me.
Ha! Forecast! You must be kidding!
We didn't really use technology forecasts.…I checked with IT yesterday and he said, "No, they were not using forecasts"…Nobody quite knows what that's going to do in the future.
…we felt we couldn't assume technology for the near future, let alone 5 or 10 years out…We knew we couldn't possibly predict technology.

One participant was quite forceful in his rejection of specific technology forecasts:

> I flatly dismiss anybody that says, "it's going to be by such and such year, you're not going to need any…" It's a crock. We've heard it too much and there's just nothing you can go on that's going to lend any credibility. It could be more, it's a crap shoot. You need to

consider both sides. If somebody's going to argue it's going to be *this* by such and such date, I'm walking away. I don't care what they're predicting.

The following statement ties back to the solution stream in an interesting way. In reference to technology forecasts:

> [We] just couldn't find any one [forecast] that we would have said, "Well, that solves it. That handles it.".… we felt that the best we could do would be to create as *flexible* [italics added] an environment, physically, technologically as we could.

As noted in the discussion of the solution stream, participants at every interview site emphasized the importance of flexibility as a criterion for weighing solutions. It was one of the most frequently noted factors in the solution stream (see Table 5) and at three sites flexibility was truly a driving factor: "One of our premises was it would be a really flexible building" and "from day one, wanted a multi-purpose building that would be extremely adaptable…we tried to make it as flexible and adaptable as possible" and "our main conversations were to remain flexible."

The drive for flexibility in the solution stream coheres with the aversion to presumed certainty in the use of technology forecasts, even—as shown in Table 7 above—among IT professionals. But as mentioned earlier, though participants at every site were reluctant to call anything they did "technology forecasting," transcripts are full of data related to decisions about the future, including the role of technology. One participant summarized the scope of the challenge of technology this way:

> [There was a long] process of determining what a library should be in these new technological times. What should our library be and once those larger questions were answered then what should a library have in it? What sizes should those things be? How many people should they serve? And really just determining how many offices are needed. How much book storage is needed currently and future? So there was at

least a year—probably a little longer than a year—of programming.

Indeed, *implicit* forecasts were made at each site that can be deduced from more general statements about the future. These statements are reviewed in the following sections on library collections, library services, and library technology.

Forecasts Relating to the Future of Library Collections

How might the future of technology affect the future of library collections? The same library director who answered "No. We figured we couldn't tell" when asked "At any point in the process, did anyone introduce a specific technology forecast as the basis for decision making related to the building?" also said the following

> We decided that we would continue to collect at the level that we currently do, if not slightly higher, which is about 3000-3500 volumes a year. We expected that print would remain one of the major resources of research for students…And we started out knowing that we were going to transfer about 250,000 volumes to the building from the old building and that sort of influenced how much space we initially built into the building and that was for us to grow without any change to the structure of the building up to 100,000 [additional] volumes which was something like 20 or 25 years.

The same kind of reasoning was used at a second site, where they assumed "that the future of collection development would proceed at or about the same pace that they had been historically and would continue at that same pace for 25 years." The implied forecast related to the effects of technology on the future of library collections is that technology would have no dramatic effect on the need to continue to grow print based collections. This then translated into very specific decisions related to the physical structure of new library buildings. This same implicit forecast was evident at every site. Table 8 is a collection of supporting statements.

Table 8: The Future of Print Library Collections
Nobody thought that print was gone…So, when we planned the building space…we were using, almost doubling the collection over 25 years. We thought print was going to be important and continuing…
…the printed book is not going anywhere for the foreseeable future, which coincides with the life of this building…regardless of the rapid growth of technology and digitalization information, we will need access to print materials for a substantial period of time.
…the migration to electronic formats for journals and other info would probably not significantly offset the imperative to collect physical text.
…in anticipation of significant growth of the print monograph collection we did additional infrastructure on floors so that in the future, compact shelving could be put in the stacks.
So we planned for print. But we also planned for electronics, making sure we had space and the ability to collect in both directions.
…we talked about just all these different issues and came to the conclusion that we would be having print during our lifetime. Big print collections still.

While emphasizing the continued growth of print resources, no participant de-emphasized technology or electronic formats. As put by one, "[W]e want to be as cutting edge technologically as possible. And I think we are. But we're not just ones to give up all the print… We don't just get rid of everything willy-nilly." In fact, each site saw the need for a pluralistic approach to the future of library collections, an intrinsically flexible approach to information formats. This was represented well in the following interview comment:

> But a couple of things that we did talk about initially were where is the future of, what's the future of the collection, is it going to be electronic, is it going to be microfilm, is it going to be print. Is it going to be a variety of formats?…we did assume all of these formats were going to continue for the foreseeable future…And certainly we didn't see any letup with people using monographs, print monographs.

Forecasts Relating to the Future of Library Services
How might the future of technology affect the future of library services? Will the need for the physical presence of library professionals in a

"brick and mortar" facility be largely offset by the transformative power of networking, information, and communication technologies that are both ubiquitous and transparent? Without downplaying the significance technological developments, participants at every site spoke with great clarity on the continued—and growing—importance of so-called traditional library services. Speaking in the context of "the circulation desk, the reference desk, all of the traditional face-to-face services" one participant captured the overall philosophy of each site: "our main value in this new building would be to put a *premium* [italics added] on those services." At another site there was the anticipation of "*large increases* [italics added] in demands for services," and from a different interview at the same site: "instead of being less necessary, it's *more necessary* [italics added]." The library director at a third site emphasized the decision that in the new building "traditional services—reference, circulation, and this sort of thing—[would be located] up front and near the entrance to the library…so that they could play a *crucial role* [italics added] in helping students…" Then, at a fourth site these services were called "extremely important" and decisions related to the new building were made with the assumption that traditional services "will continue to remain the *backbone* [italics added] regardless of the format of the collection."

The phrase "high tech high touch" popularized by the writings of futurist John Naisbitt[11] and applied to librarianship by Lynn Jurewicz and Todd Cutler[12] is an appropriate moniker for the mindset toward library services across all interviews. This is especially evident in this comment from the fifth site:

> [W]e wound up designing a service desk that was circular but broken into four quadrants so that traffic could flow through. The idea being [that] librarians would invite students to come behind the desk and work with them at one of four workstations to sit down in a more comfortable environment.

This theme is again repeated by another participant:

> I really worked for good people spaces. We worked for spaces where students could collaborate. We worked for spaces where students could have interviews with

research librarians. We have a very very people service oriented arrangement.…Lots of face-to-face services. We also do the whole range of virtual reference and phone reference and document delivery…

At one library, the new reference desk is staffed by professional librarians *and* IT technicians and at another site a participant spoke in the same breath about their new campus wide library book delivery service and their new library based "digital media studio [with] one-on-one assistance.…geared to students for working with them on multimedia projects." These decision makers illustrate a keen awareness of the principle articulated by Naisbitt: "Whenever institutions introduce new technology…they should build in a high-touch component; if they don't, people will try to create their own or reject the new technology."13

Forecasts Relating to the Future of Library Technology
How might the future of technology affect the future of library technology? This question is so bound with the matter of technology forecasts that a clean disaggregation is not easy. Participant perspectives were very positive about library technology in general and very nondescript in their comments about what the future of library technology might look like. For instance,

> [W]e just decided we were going to be cutting edge and then we had to go about defining what cutting edge was. We wanted great technology. We wanted learning technology, teaching technology, research technology, administrative technology. We wanted technology.

At another site, a participant said "we were obviously trapped in the middle of an IT revolution—and we had no idea exactly which direction that was going to go." An experience at a previous place of employment tempered the approach of another participant:

> [W]hen I was at the University of Virginia, they were building a research building, the fourth of a line in medical research buildings, aptly named medical research four. When that building was completed, it

had to be gutted because as technology had changed, the things they were planning on doing in there were no longer in vogue. And it had to be gutted and had to be redesigned, interior-wise, for something different.

So, whereas another library director observed that there was no doubt that the new library "was going to be loaded with technology" she also noted that

We knew we couldn't possibly predict technology, so we tried to provide adequate wiring, electricity, wireless, and space for the addition of any new technologies, rather than plan for what they were. This made us feel confident that as things changed, the building could change to meet that need.

This same mindset—to be prepared for change—is evident from an interview at another site as well:

[F]rankly, we didn't really know where the technology was going to take it but we wanted rooms where we could get the best and latest technology where our faculty and staff could learn and students could learn the technology. Or use assistance in learning how to use it. And the space is flexible enough in terms of free-floating furniture as technology changes or other teaching techniques change, we would have the ability to have a resource room that could respond to those changes in technology.

Participants at every site affirmed the tension between a conviction that library technology is vital to library operations and services but that the future of library technology is indecipherable.

Conclusion

Findings from this research confirm the descriptive rigor of the decision making model of Cohen et al. and Kingdon. The model is comprehensive enough that conspicuous outliers are virtually absent. The model is also remarkably parsimonious. Insight into research data is possible through four primary organizing concepts: participants, problems, solutions, and coupling. Finally, the model is uniquely heuristic, framing its organizing concepts in a thoroughly counterintuitive manner, leading to insights that other models of decision making cannot provide.

Library directors and other key decision making participants describe the use of technology forecasts during the construction of new academic libraries in uniformly agnostic terms. Nonetheless, while studiously avoiding the *term* "forecasting," they were deeply involved in the estimation of conditions related to the future effects of technology—especially with respect to impact of technology on collections, services, and library technology *per se*. Forecasts were made, but only implicitly.

Notes

1. Cohen, March, and Olsen, "A Garbage Can Model of Organizational Choice," 16.
2. Kingdon, *Agendas, Alternatives, and Public Policies*, 202.
3. March, *A Primer on Decision Making: How Decisions Happen*, 205.
4. Lucker, "Negotiating the Rocky Shoals: The Politics of Building a Library," 23. Dr. Lucker has affirmed that, in his experience, the same percentage holds for the years since 1991 (personal communication, February 21, 2008).
5. Kingdon, *Agendas, Alternatives, and Public Policies*, 85.
6. Cohen, March, and Olsen, "A Garbage Can Model of Organizational Choice," 3.
7. March, *A Primer on Decision Making: How Decisions Happen*, 205.
8. Martino, "Technological Forecasting: An Introduction," 13.
9. Two databases (ERIC and Library, Information Science, & Technology Abstracts) were selected based on their coverage of library related literature, a replicable database search protocol was formulated, a bibliography was generated from the search results, and "false hits" (results not relevant to the search) were culled by reading the abstract for each item in the bibliography. All of the remaining 1,317 abstracts were copied and imported into NVIVO7, a software program used for research involving qualitative text analysis. Each abstract was read and categorized according forecast content. From this, a simple tally of frequencies was compiled.
10. Silverman, *Doing Qualitative Research*, 220.
11. Naisbitt, *Megatrends*.
12. Jurewicz and Cutler, *High Tech, High Touch: Library Customer Service Through Technology*.
13. Naisbitt, *Megatrends*.

Making Peace With Ambiguity

The decision making described in this research was often messy and painful. The stock portrayal of planning and decision making as deliberative engagement of a manageably stable—though perhaps unruly—environment is usurped by a picture of reflexive heuristics in an unpredictably fluid environment. Yet within the complexity, unpredictability, and uncontrollability of institutional decision settings, general patterns can be discerned, opportunities may be realized, and meaningful progress is possible.

This research explored the process of decision making during the construction of new academic libraries at American universities, with special attention to the influence of technology forecasts. The conceptual framework for this study was the garbage can model of decision making and technology forecasts were viewed through the lens of the anticipated effects of technology on library collections, library services, and library technology.

The findings of this research support the descriptive rigor of the garbage can model, sometimes in surprising ways. For instance, as noted earlier, none of the five directors named a vice president for academics or provost for inclusion in the decision making cohort and only one of the twenty participants named a provost among those who were perceived to be significantly influential during the library construction process. This is surprising since, as the chief executive level officer in most library reporting lines, the provost would be a natural candidate for a heavy level of involvement and influence during a project as consequential as the construction of a new library. The bureaucratic decision making model would almost require the provost to take a strong place in the process. But true to the garbage can model, decision making participation was thoroughly fluid and, in the case of provosts, counterintuitive.

A second surprising finding was the sheer absence of formal forecasting of any sort. The rational model would predict just the opposite. This, too, supports the descriptive rigor of the garbage can model. Decision making was a matter of the temporal sorting of variables leading to serendipitous coupling *in the present* instead of rationally deduced conclusions based on firm visions of the future.

One final surprise is worth noting. The original garbage can model was proposed by Cohen et al. nearly forty years ago, long before the internet and ubiquitous digital technology. Yet the model seems *particularly* suited to decision making in this new environment. What is our contemporary technological setting if it is not an organized anarchy? Perhaps the model really does apprehend a substrate of the human condition. Different accessory features may be observed depending on the decision setting, as in this study, but the core tenets remain as a relevant conceptual framework.

A variety of further conclusions are possible for both decision making and forecasting. These are discussed in the following sections.

Decision Making

The decision making described in this research was often messy and painful. Indeed, the boilerplate version of decision making—i.e. 1) define the problem, 2) identify the solution, and 3) engage decision makers—is turned on its head by the garbage can model. In this model, there is no set of consistently ordered steps that describes how decisions actually take place. So, in fact, "few truly strategic decisions are made in the context of a formal process."[1]

Instead, the primary variables—problems, solutions, and decision making participants—coexist in a fluid relationship to one another. Likewise, *how* something acquires the status of "problem" or "solution" is not a matter of ordered steps based on an objectively described state of affairs. Something *becomes* a problem or a solution based on many factors that also coexist in a fluid relationship to one another.

The way decision making participants interpret these many factors at any point in time determines whether the combination of problems, solutions, and active decision makers makes a decision possible. But participants come and go from decision making settings both physically and mentally, and institutional priorities shift on a regular basis.

Hence, the mix of participants, problems, and solutions is in constant flux. When the right combination of participants, problems, and solutions converge, a decision may occur but the timing of the convergence and the factors that bring it to pass are complex, unpredictable, and uncontrollable.

At first, the observation that the dynamics of university decision making involve the coming together of problems, solutions, and participants—and that some key participants behave in entrepreneurial ways—may seem too plainly patent to even mention. But, quoting University of Virginia professor E. D. Hirsch from another context: "This would seem to be trivial, but trivial truths can imply far from trivial conclusions."[2] The genius—the far from trivial quality—of the garbage can model is the thoroughly counterintuitive weight it assigns to the relative *independence* of problems, solutions, and participants, and the way they flow through the university in complex, unpredictable, uncontrollable, even obtuse ways. The stock portrayal of planning and decision making as deliberative engagement of a manageably stable—though perhaps unruly—environment is usurped by a picture of reflexive heuristics in an unpredictably fluid environment. On the whole, decisions—especially large scale decisions—happen through temporal sorting and serendipitous coupling instead of being rationally determined. Other decision making models, such as political or collegial, may have occasional cameo appearances during the process on a micro level. For periods of time they may even have some degree of dominance on the macro level. But none can claim a persistently leading or *causal* role at all times and places. Perhaps this partially accounts for the surprise of rational model adherents when well laid plans go awry, the disappointment of collegial model adherents when others manipulate instead of cooperate, the confusion of bureaucratic model adherents when carefully articulated policies and procedures fail to address a decision making scenario, and the frustration of political model adherents when brilliant maneuvering through the system leads to a backwater cul-de-sac.

Cohen et al. described institutional decision making settings as "organized anarchies."[3] At points the question arises: "Why bother?" Does all of this mean that the life of a decision maker is no more than an endless bumper car ride? This is an existentially tempting, though overdrawn, conclusion. Even in the original exposition of the garbage can model by Cohen et al. *pure* anarchy is not in view. An environment that is complex, unpredictable, and uncontrollable need not be pervasively erratic. Thus, while affirming the organized anarchy view of the American federal government, Kingdon noted that "we will find our emphasis being placed more on the 'organized' than on the 'anarchy' as we discover structures and patterns in the processes."[4]

So, within the complexity, unpredictability, and uncontrollability of institutional decision settings, general patterns can be discerned, opportunities may be realized, and meaningful progress is possible. Strikingly beautiful libraries—sources of immense benefit—now stand on each of the campuses studied for this research. Consider the observations in Table 9.

Table 9: Why Bother With Decision Making?
[S]tudents came into the old building because they had to, and students come into the new building because they want to.
We're seeing more use of databases, more traffic through the gate, more interaction with the library.
[I]t's been unbelievable the transformation…It brought new life to the academic program…It's a very inspiring building and it just fits well on our campus and it has taken us to the next level where we want to go.
The building has far surpassed our expectations in some respects. I don't think anyone realized how much that building would be used.
I'm amazed by how much it boosts morale to be in this building.
[I]t's been unbelievable the transformation…It brought new life to the academic program.

One more poignant observation from a participant is worth including:

> Just last night I was coming out of a faculty senate [meeting] and I was walking out and the library was in front of us. One of the faculty members [was] with me. We were commenting on what a surprisingly lovely evening it was. It was like 5:30, the sky was clear. It was kind of twilighty. And [the faculty member said] look at your building, isn't your building beautiful? And I think yes. I still walk up to it sometimes—Oh look at it. It makes me so happy.

Certainly, though the garbage can process "violates standard no-tions of how decisions ought to be made"[5], the ability to make decisions with rewarding effects is not wholly eclipsed.

So, what is the meaning of these findings? More to the point, "How should a decision maker behave in a garbage can world?"[6] The begin-ning of an answer to this question is that resignation to the ambiguity of the process really *is* an endless bumper car ride, but a certain kind of patient and forgiving resolve can yield rewarding results.

First, a measured approach to the insights of other decision making models is appropriate even if none can claim supremacy as a fully de-scriptive framework. A sober awareness of the limits of other models of decision making can enable a sagacious approach to their tenets without falling prey to a misunderstanding of what decision making actually involves. Strive to be rational without the presumption of full comprehen-sion (the rational model); write clear policies and procedures but only in pencil (bureaucratic); use personal influence to affect institutional process but without overestimating or overvaluing your power (political); involve stakeholders at every turn but do not ignore the presence and negative potential of hidden agendas, distended egos, and ill-formed opinions (col-legial). Strive for clarity but, when necessary, make peace with ambiguity.

Second, assume an entrepreneurial approach to institutional life. Be alert, flexible, proactive, and patient.

Third, for library directors and deans, be a student of how the library fits within the patterns of broader decision streams at the university. No library is—or at least should not be—an island.

Finally, adopt a vision for decision making that is based more on a process like long distance off-path hiking in the Appalachian Moun-tains than on driving from Dallas to Houston. Institutional decision making is more a matter of disciplined orienteering over perpetually changing terrain and less a matter of using an online mapping service or dashboard GPS to plot a route along established pathways.

Forecasting

Burnham Beckwith, a social scientist writing during the mid-twentieth century, offered the following in the preface to his book on the future:

> The hunger for foreknowledge is age-old and univer-

sal. The theory that events and trends can be reliably predicted by scientific methods is relatively new and little known....In this book I shall set forth the most significant long-run historical trends which will continue or arise during the next *five hundred years and which now are scientifically predictable [italics added]*.[7]

In contrast, at the beginning of the twenty-first century Michael Crosbie—an architect—and Damon Hickey—an academic librarian—noted that one of the top factors affecting the construction of new academic libraries is "uncertainty about the future."[8] As noted earlier in the findings section, this uncertainty was copiously reflected in the interviews for this research. For instance, asked about specific technology forecasts used as the basis for decision making related to the building, one library director replied: "Ha! Forecast! You must be kidding!"

Interview transcripts for this research are full of data related to decisions about the future—including the role of technology—but participants were uniformly reluctant to call anything they did "technology forecasting." So even if "all decisions are about the future"[9], not all decision makers in this study adopted a forecasting vocabulary to describe what they did during the construction of libraries.

The roots of this ambivalence, this making of forecasts without making *forecasts*, might be explained—at least in part—by psychologist David Loye who noted that the accuracy of a prediction "is heavily dependent on whether there is a fixity or fluidity of social pattern and on the predictor's placement in the extension of this social patterning through time."[10] The participants in this study were involved in the early planning stages for the libraries that were built at points in time immediately prior to, during, and following the "dot com" stock market crash—when mountains of technology forecasts fell like a house of cards[11]—as well as the events subsequent to September 11, 2001. The broad social patterning within which these participants built libraries was characterized by disruptive fluidity. One library director offered these comments on the effect of September 11, 2001: "we thought we'd just close up shop and go find a cave to live in. We had a building committee meeting that morning and we couldn't even focus." Participant attitudes toward technology forecasts indicate a response to an environment of such sweeping uncertainty that subjective confidence in forecasts was unachievable.

Yet the future continues to beckon and decision makers are compelled to envision the path ahead. The power of a forecast, by whatever name, to inform thoughts about the future and to influence decision making in the present *remains* a topic worthy of reflection. But contrary to Beckwith—who in 1967 claimed that scientifically precise prediction was possible for up to five hundred years into the future—Jantsch, also in 1967, was more prescient for his time as well as ours: "technological forecasting is not yet a science but an art, and is characterized today by attitudes, not tools."[12]

Indeed, for all the literature available on forecasting techniques, not a single interview participant described the use of formal forecasting methods. In part, this might be explained by one of the common features of the academic library mission, to preserve the *past* intellectual record of a culture. But even preservation has a forward thinking element. How shall the library transmit and give access to the intellectual record—in all its various formats—to each *future* generation? And so the question of why there was an absence of formal forecasting among participants remains.

The garbage can model offers insight at just this point because a forecast implicitly relies upon the assumptions of the rational and political models of decision making. In its pure form, for a forecast to "work" the scope of knowledge required by the rational model and the power to effect required by the political model must be undiluted. But no such world exists. Forecasts fair poorly in a garbage can world. But as noted earlier, there was a strong drive for flexibility in the solution stream. In fact, the category "flexibility" was the third most frequent in the interviews and it appeared in more interviews overall than any other category in the solution stream. So instead of using forecasts to artificially *reduce* the existential tension of uncertainty about the future, participants pursued flexibility to *increase* the practical ability to be nimble as the future unfolds. The meaning of this for decision makers includes the possibility that informed agnosticism with an emphasis on flexibility—like that of the interview participants for this research—is a prudent response to technology forecasts and the challenge of decision making in general.

A New Metaphor for the Garbage Can Model?

In their groundbreaking work on metaphor, Lakoff and Johnson contend that the role of metaphor in defining conceptual systems is highly consequential:

> The concepts that govern our thought are not just matters of the intellect. They also govern everyday functioning, down to the most mundane details. Our concepts structure what we perceive, how we get around in the world, and how we relate to other people. Our conceptual system thus plays a central role in defining our everyday realities. If we are right in suggesting that our conceptual system is largely metaphorical, then the way we think, what we experience, and what we do every day is very much a matter of metaphor.[13]

As a construct for understanding decision making, the garbage can model provides descriptive insights offered by no other model. The garbage can *metaphor* for the model opens ways to think about how the model applies to decision making. But the hazard of a metaphor is that it can *constrain* thinking as well.

The original article by Cohen et al. actually offers a mixed metaphor for the model. The "garbage can" name for the model is explained in terms of a different kind of metaphor, "streams." Of course, things do come and go from a garbage can; they flow in and out. But garbage cans and streams *as metaphors* are drawn from two different realms of experience. A garbage can is a mechanical device and a stream is a natural phenomenon. This may seem like a hairsplitting distinction but perhaps the power of a compound metaphor is enhanced if there is a normal continuity between the metaphors. Mixed metaphors work, but only with some effort, constraining their power to stimulate the imagination. So too with garbage cans and streams.

Streams are part of a natural ecosystem, not a large garbage can. And the characteristics of the streams in the garbage can model are more similar to streams in nature than the relatively static objects normally found in garbage cans—streams are in *constant* flux. A more helpful rubric for the model might be based on consistently ecological metaphors. At one point, March himself used an ecological metaphor to describe the garbage can process. He described decision making as "an ecology of actors trying to act rationally with limited knowledge and preference coherence; trying to discover and execute proper behavior in ambiguous situations; and trying to discover, construct, and communicate interpretations of a confusing world."[14]

In the field of biology, ecology is the study of the "pattern of relations between organisms and their environment."[15] Sociologists have applied the ecological metaphor as a name for a field of study, human ecology: "a branch of sociology dealing especially with the spatial and temporal interrelationships between humans and their economic, social, and political organization."[16] Many students of human ecology focus on the interrelationship between human populations and biological ecosystems.[17] For instance, Glover studied the effect of exotic weeds on cultural change in Papua New Guinea.[18] But other scholars have applied the concept of human ecology to other domains: psychology[19], natural childbirth[20], and disability and the incidence of poverty.[21] Nardi and O'Day even applied the ecological metaphor to libraries: "a library is an information ecology."[22]

As an alternative construct, an ecological model of decision making might suggest new ways to explore decision making phenomena. As a derivative of the garbage can model, an ecological model could preserve all of the insights of the garbage can model while providing new metaphorical categories. Additional insights may open in unexpected, serendipitous ways.

Notes

1. Kaplan and Beinhocker, "The Real Value of Strategic Planning," 71.
2. Hirsch, *Validity in Interpretation,* 134.
3. Cohen, March, and Olsen, "A Garbage Can Model of Organizational Choice," 2.
4. Kingdon, *Agendas, Alternatives, and Public Policies,* 86.
5. Cohen, March, and Olsen, "A Garbage Can Model of Organizational Choice," 11.
6. March, *A Primer on Decision Making: How Decisions Happen,* 205.
7. Beckwith, *The Next 500 Years: Scientific Predictions of Major Social Trends,* ix, x.
8. Crosbie and Hickey, *When Change is Set in Stone, 17.*
9. Boulding, "Forward," v.
10. Loye, *The Knowable Future: A Psychology of Forecasting and Prophecy,* 120.
11. cf. Bahr, "Library Buildings in a Digital Age."
12. Jantsch, *Technological Forecasting in Perspective,* 17.

13. Lakoff and Johnson, *Metaphors We Live By*, 3.
14. March, "How Decisions Happen in Organizations," 111.
15. Mish, *Merriam-Webster's Collegiate Dictionary*, 10th ed., 365.
16. Ibid., 564.
17. Ishisaka, "Human Ecology: The Interaction of Man With His Ecosystem."
18. Glover, "Exotic Weeds and Cultural Change."
19. Insel and Moos, "Psychological Environments: Expanding the Scope of Human Ecology."
20. Mansfield, "The Social Nature of Childbirth."
21. Saunders, "The Costs of Disability and the Incidence of Poverty."
22. Nardi and O'Day, *Information Ecologies: Using Technology With Heart*, 49.

Research Design

Overview of Method

The methodology for this research explored four questions through two approaches to data collection. The four research questions were:

1. For the period 1990-2007, what were the most frequently published forecasts related to technology in libraries?
2. How do library directors and other key decision making participants describe decision making during the construction of new academic libraries?
3. How do library directors and other key decision making participants describe the use of technology forecasts during the construction of new academic libraries?
4. What additional internal and external elements influenced decision making during the construction of new academic libraries?

Data were culled from both published literature and transcribed interviews. Lakoff and Johnson noted that

> [O]ur conceptual system is not something we are normally aware of. In most of the little things we do every day, we simply think and act more or less automatically along certain lines. Just what these lines are is by no means obvious. One way to find out is by looking at language. Since communication is based on the same conceptual system that we use in thinking and acting, language is an important source of evidence for what that system is like.[1]

Two varieties of language were analyzed for this research. For research question one, formal (written) language recorded in periodical literature abstracts is described. For research questions two, three, and four, informal (spoken) language recorded in interview transcripts were examined. The topic, recently completed library construction projects, provided a context of decision making that was highly focused, highly consequential, and highly memorable to participants.

Research Question One

For this question, databases were selected based on coverage of library related literature, a replicable database search protocol was formulated, a bibliography was generated from the search results, "false hits" (results not relevant to the search) were culled by reading the abstract for each item in the bibliography, the abstract text of the remaining items were analyzed through the forecast lens and a taxonomy—with simple frequency notes for each taxonomic element—was developed.

The databases used for this research were ERIC and LISTA. ERIC (Educational Resource Information Center), the premier database for research in education, covers more that 1,000 education related publications dating back to the mid-1960s. LISTA (Library, Information Science, & Technology Abstracts) is one of four primary databases for research related to libraries. Two of the others—Library and Information Science Abstracts (LISA) and Library Literature & Information Science Full Text—do not focus as heavily on technology and so LISTA was the natural choice over these. The third library related database—Library Literature & Information Science Retrospective—covers the years 1905-1983, the wrong time frame for this study. LISTA indexes more than 600 sources from the mid-1960s to present. A further advantage to ERIC and LISTA is that a federated search is possible through EBSCO, a database vendor service. A federated search is one in which two or more databases are searched simultaneously and results are unduplicated; where the databases locate the same bibliographic item, it is presented only once in the result list. This saves the researcher from the intensive labor of searching databases one by one and then manually culling through hundreds—or thousands—of items in order to obtain a single list of unique entries.

Since both ERIC and LISTA are abstract databases, the full text of all abstracts for articles written between 1990 and late 2007 were searched using the query: (future* or trend* or predict* or forecast*) AND (tech* or digit* or electron* or internet or web) AND (college* or universit* or academic) AND (librar*). The asterisk is a "wild card" character that allows the retrieval of all words with the letters preceding the asterisk. Thus, for example, universit* will retrieve both university and universities. This protocol produced a list of 1317 abstracts.

Research Questions Two, Three, and Four

In-depth recorded interviews, using a semi-structured question protocol, was the data collection methodology for these questions. Interviewing is appropriate to these questions due to its established relevance to the goal of capturing the meaning of experience in people's own words.[2] As put by Seidman, "at the root of in-depth interviewing is an interest in understanding the experience of other people and the meaning they make of that experience."[3] Woike adds "by asking people directly what they think and feel, we know about their cognitive representation of their thoughts and feelings and what sorts of information are important to them, rather than those of the researcher."[4] In-depth interviewing is particularly applicable to the exploration of decision making because "a basic assumption in in-depth interviewing research is that the meaning people make of their experience affects the way they carry out that experience."[5] The incorporation of a forecast into the decision making process endows the forecast with meaning in that context. Interviewing decision makers who interact with forecasts is a way to discover the meaning of a forecast from their perspective.

Interviewees were chosen through purposive sampling, a method whereby "participants are selected according to predetermined criteria relevant to a particular research objective."[6] Participants were drawn from a geographically diverse selection of library directors and their primary decision making cohorts who completed the construction of new libraries between 2005 and 2007, identified through the annual description of new academic library building projects published by *Library Journal. Research by Guest, Bunce, and Johnson*[7] details evidence that twelve interviews is sufficient to obtain saturation, the point "when each additional interviewee adds little to what you have already learned."[8] For this study, library directors from five campuses were selected—along with three to four members of the decision making cohort they identified—resulting in twenty interviews.

Interviews were taped and transcribed; transcripts were analyzed and comments were categorized. Due to the distant geographical location of participants, recorded telephone interviews were used. Though the use of telephone interviews is not the dominant means of collecting qualitative interview data,[9] neither is it an uncommon practice.[10] Despite variety in terms of geographical location and institutional profile, this sample still provides enough homogeneity to enable comparability between participants and to suggest transferability to other library settings based on substantive *a priori commonalities between all types of academic libraries*.[11] The geographically diverse scope of the sample ensures a high level of interest to a wide number of readers and researchers.

Because "the participant's perspective on the phenomenon of interest should unfold as the participant views it, not as the researcher views it"[12] the interview protocol was used as a guide to the discussion, not a rigid checklist. Consequently, additional questions were occasionally posed when new insights emerged during the interviews. Interview questions were developed following pilot interviews during which phrasing and content was refined in light of comments made during the interviews. Two library directors served as pilot participants, each of which has completed major library building projects in recent years.

Access to interview participants was arranged through personal requests by letters of invitation with a telephone follow up. Two letter formats were used, one for library directors and deans and another for their decision making cohort. Interviews were scheduled at times convenient for the participants during work hours, providing a comfortable and convenient setting. Tape-recorded interviews, lasting approximately 45 to 60 minutes, were transcribed for analysis. Transcripts were then coded and examined for patterns and themes using NVIVO7, a software program used for qualitative text analysis.

Data Analysis

The method for data analysis in this study is qualitative content analysis based upon responses to open-ended questions from a semi-structured interview protocol. Woike contends that "by asking people to write or express orally their thoughts and reactions, it is possible to discover unique patterns of expression that would be extremely difficult to capture" by other research methods; consequently, "many researchers find content coding of open-ended responses to be an invaluable tool."[13] Content analysis is "a technique for systematically describing the form and content of written or spoken material;"[14] it is "a systematic, rigorous approach to analyzing documents obtained or generated in the course of research,"[15] and "the result of a qualitative content analysis is an inclusive representation of patterns found in a corpus."[16] Content analysis allows the comparison of trends over time, is generally marked by ease of replication, and is flexible in terms of quantitative or qualitative approaches.[17]

Analysis of the periodical literature used for this study was limited to a topical compilation of technology forecasts related to academic libraries as reflected in database article abstracts. As noted above, a taxonomy of these forecasts—with simple frequency counts for each taxonomic element—was developed.

Analysis of the interview transcripts was pursued in a "directed" fashion[18] as a recursive search for patterns and meaning within the data. In "directed" content analysis, the researcher "starts with a theory or relevant research findings as guidance for initial codes."[19] These codes serve as "heuristic devices for discovery."[20] Then, "operational definitions for each category are determined using the theory."[21] After coding the data with the predetermined codes, "data that cannot be coded are identified and analyzed later to determine if they represent a new category or a subcategory of an existing code."[22] Finally, "the theory or prior research used will guide the discussion of findings. Newly identified categories either offer a contradictory view of the phenomenon or might further refine, extend, or enrich the theory."[23] For this research, patterns and themes indicative of garbage can decision making are highlighted as well as features in the data not foreshadowed by garbage can assumptions. Every effort was made to express findings in terms that respect the substance of participants' reflections.

Data Quality

Miles and Huberman[24] offer a survey of approaches for assessing qualitative research. Based on their survey, data quality for this study is demonstrated in the following ways.

First, this research meets the standards of replicability and confirmability. The "study's general methods and procedures" are "described explicitly and in detail;" it is possible to "follow the actual sequence of how data were collected, processed, condensed/transformed, and displayed for specific conclusion drawing;" conclusions are "explicitly linked with exhibits of condensed/displayed data;" and the data are "retained and available for reanalysis by others."[25]   Second, this research meets the standards of reliability, dependability, and auditability. The research questions are clear and "the features of the study design are congruent with them;" "findings show meaningful parallelism across data sources;" "analytic constructs" are "clearly specified;" and data were collected across a wide range of "appropriate settings, times, and respondents."[26]

Third, this research meets the standards of credibility and authenticity. Descriptions of the data are "context rich;" "data sources produce generally converging conclusions;" data are "well linked to the categories of prior theory;" "measures reflect the constructs in play;" and "areas of uncertainty" are identified.[27]

Fourth, this research meets the standards of transferability and fittingness. The "characteristics of the original sample of persons, settings, processes" are "fully described enough to permit adequate comparisons with other samples;" "possible threats to generalizability" are acknowledged; the "scope and boundaries of reasonable generalization from the study" are described; the sampling is "theoretically diverse enough to encourage broader applicability;" "the findings are confirmatory of prior theory;" and the study suggests "settings where the findings could be fruitfully tested further."[28]

Finally, this research meets the standards of application and action orientation. Findings "stimulate 'working hypotheses' on the part of the reader as guidance for future action."[29]

Limitations

This study is limited by participant profession (academic library directors and other higher education decision makers), institutional profile (colleges and universities), geography (five of fifty states), time frame (1990-2007 for periodical article abstracts; 2006-2007 for building projects; calendar 2008 for interviews), and researcher subjectivity. These limits are not so narrow, however, to prevent other kinds of academic professionals in colleges and universities elsewhere from garnering helpful insights.

Furthermore, findings from this research suggest directions for further study of a rarely examined topic. Future research might use the insights from this study as a model to give form to data collected in other libraries or in other institutional subcultures related to libraries.

A better understanding of decision making and how we think about the future promises to provide a means to greater clarity and focus for higher education professionals.

Notes

1. Lakoff and Johnson, *Metaphors We Live By*, 3.
2. Marshall and Rossman, *Designing Qualitative Research*, 3rd ed., 61.
3. Seidman, *Interviewing as Qualitative Research*, 3.
4. Woike, "Content Coding of Open-ended Questions," 306.
5. Seidman, *Interviewing as Qualitative Research*, 4.
6. Guest, Bunce, and Johnson, "How Many Interviews Are Enough?," 61.
7. Guest, Bunce, and Johnson, "How Many Interviews Are Enough?."
8. Rubin and Rubin, *Qualitative Interviewing: The Art of Hearing Data*, 72.
9. Ibid., 141.
10. Telephone interviews have been used to study decision making related to consumer behavior (Huang, Wolfe, and Mckissick, "Consumers' Willingness to Pay for Irradiated Poultry Products"), medical decisions (Vig et al., "Surviving Surrogate Decision Making") and college recruitment practices (Norris, "Pawns or Professionals: The 21st Century Admissions Counselor").
11. A function of both mimetic and normative profession driven isomorphism—i.e. copycat behavior—identified by DiMaggio and Powell, "The Iron Cage Revisited."
12. Marshall and Rossman, *Designing Qualitative Research*, 3rd ed., 108.
13. Woike, "Content Coding of Open-ended Questions," 293.
14. Sommer and Sommer, *A Practical Guide to Behavioral Research*, 177.
15. White and Marsh, "Content Analysis: A Flexible Methodology," 22.
16. Thompson, "Collaboration in Technical Communication," 162.
17. Sommer and Sommer, *A Practical Guide to Behavioral Research*, 179.
18. Hseih and Shannon, "Three Approaches to Qualitative Content Analysis."
19. Ibid., 1277; cf. Taylor-Powell and Renner, *Analyzing Qualitative Data*, 3; Merriam, *Qualitative Research and Case Study Applications in Education*, 2nd ed., 182; Coffey and Atkinson, *Making Sense of Qualitative Data*, 31, 32.
20. Seidel & Kelle, "Different Functions of Coding in the Analysis of Textual Data," 58.
21. Hseih and Shannon, "Three Approaches to Qualitative Content Analysis," 1281.
22. Ibid., 1282.
23. Ibid., 1283.
24. Miles and Huberman, *Qualitative Data Analysis: An Expanded Sourcebook*, 2nd ed., 277–280.
25. Ibid., 278.
26. Ibid.
27. Ibid., 279.
28. Ibid.
29. Ibid., 280.

Bibliography

Adams, Roy J. *Information Technology & Libraries: A future for Academic Libraries*. Dover: Croom Helm, 1986.

Advertisement for Telex. *The Economist* 179 (1956): 867.

Allain, Violet A. *Futuristics and Education*. Bloomington: Phi Delta Kappa Educational Foundation, 1979.

Arms, Carolyn R. "The Technological Context." *In Campus Strategies for Libraries and Electronic Information,* edited by Carolyn R. Arms, 11–35. Bedford: Digital Press, 1990.

Asheim, Lester. *The Future of the Book. Chicago:* University of Chicago Graduate Library School, 1955.

Augier, Mie. "James March on Education, Leadership, and Don Quixote: Introduction and Interview." *Academy of Management Learning and Education* 3 (2004): 169–177.

Babcock, J. G. "Special Material in Libraries." *News Notes of California Libraries* 14 (1919): 155–156.

Bahr, Alice H. "Library Buildings in a Digital Age, Why Bother?" *College & Research Libraries News* 61 (2000): 590–591.

Baines, Anna. "Management Forecasting." *Work Study* 41 (1992): 6–9.

Baldridge, John V. *Power and Conflict in the University: Research in the Sociology of Complex Organizations*. New York: John Wiley, 1971.

Baldridge, John V., D. V. Curtis, G. P. Ecker, and G. L. Riley. "Alternative Models of Governance in Higher Education." In *ASHE Reader on Organization and Governance in Higher Education*, edited by M. Peterson, 34–49. Needham Heights: Ginn Press, 1991.

Barry, David, Catherine D. Cramton, and Stephen J. Carroll. "Navigating the Garbage Can: How Agendas Help Managers Cope With Job Realities." *Academy of Management Executive*, 11 (1997): 26–42.

Battin, Patricia. "The Electronic Library—A Vision for the Future." *EDUCOM Bulletin* 19 (1984): 12–17, 34.

Baylis, Thomas A. *Governing by Committee: Collegial Leadership in Advanced Societies.* Albany: State University of New York Press, 1989.

Beach, Lee R. and Terry Connolly. *The Psychology of Decision Making: People in Organizations,* 2nd ed. Thousand Oaks: Sage, 2005.

Becker, Joseph. "The Future of Library Automation and Information Networks." In *Library Automation: A State of the Art Review,* edited by Stephen R. Salmon, 3–12. Chicago: American Library Association, 1969.

Beckwith, Burnham P. *The Next 500 Years: Scientific Predictions of Major Social Trends.* New York: Exposition Press, 1967.

Bennett, Scott. "Campus Cultures Fostering Literacy." *Portal: Libraries and the Academy* 7 (2007): 147–167.

Bennett, Scott. "The Choice for Learning." *Journal of Academic Librarianship* 32 (2006): 3–13.

Bennett, Scott. "First Questions for Designing Higher Education Learning Spaces." *Journal of Academic Librarianship* 33 (2007): 14–26.

Bennett, Scott. "Libraries and Learning: A History of Paradigm Change." *Portal: Libraries and the Academy* 9 (2009): 181–197.

Bennett, Scott. *Libraries Designed for Learning.* Washington DC: Council on Library and Information Resources, 2003.

Bennett, Scott. "Righting the Balance." In *The Library as Place: Changes in Learning Patterns, Collections, Technology and Use,* edited by Geoffrey T. Freeman, 10–24. Washington DC: Council on Library Resources, 2005.

Bertman, Stephen. *Hyperculture: The Cost of Human Speed.* Westport, CT: Praeger, 1998.

Biocca, Frank A. "The Pursuit of Sound: Radio, Perception, and Utopia in the Early Twentieth Century." *Media Culture and Society* 10 (1988): 61–79.

Bogart, Dave. *The Bowker Annual: Library and Book Trade Almanac,* 48th ed. Medford: Information Today, 2003.

Bolling, G. Frederic. *The Art of Forecasting.* Brookfield: Gower, 1996.

Bolman, Lee G. and Terrence E. Deal. *Reframing Organizations: Artistry, Choice, and Leadership,* 3rd ed., San Francisco: Jossey-Bass, 2003.

Boseman, Barry and William E. McAlpine. "Goals and Bureaucratic Decision Making: An Experiment." *Human Relations* 30 (1977): 417–429.

Boulding, K. "Forward." In *The Image of the Future*, edited by Fred Polak and Elise Boulding, v–vi. New York: Elsevier, 1973.

Boynton, Andrew C. and Robert W. Zmud. "Information Technology Planning for the 1990's: Directions for Practice and Research." *MIS Quarterly* 11 (1987): 58–71.

Branscomb, Lewis M. *The Electronic Library. Journal of Communication*, 31 (1981):143–150.

Breivik, Patricia S. and E. Gordon Gee. *Higher Education in the Internet Age: Libraries Creating a Strategic Edge.* Westport: American Council on Education, 2006.

Brockhoff, Klaus. "Decision Quality and Information." In *Empirical Research on Organizational Decision Making*, edited by Eberhard Witte and Hans-Jürgen Zimmerman, 249–265. New York: Elsevier, 1986.

Brown, James D. "Cataloguing Appliances." *Library* 3 (1891): 393.

Bryson, John M. Strategic Planning for Public and Nonprofit Organizations. San Francisco: Jossey-Bass, 1995.

Buchanan, Leigh and Andre O'Connell. "A Brief History of Decision Making." *Harvard Business Review* 84 (2006): 32–41.

Buschman, John. "Librarians, Self-censorship, and Information Technologies." *College & Research Libraries* 55 (1994): 221–228.

Buschman, John. "On Libraries and the Public Sphere." *Library Philosophy and Practice* 7 (2005): 1–8.

Cady, Susan A. "The Electronic Revolution in Libraries: Microfilm Déjà vu?" *College & Research Libraries*, 51 (1990): 374–386.

Caldwell, Dan. "Bureaucratic Foreign Policy Making." *American Behavioral Scientist* 21 (1977): 87–110.

Cantril, Hadley. "The Prediction of Social Events." *Journal of Abnormal and Social Psychology* 33 (1938): 364–389.

Chaffee, Ellen E. *Rational Decision Making in Higher Education*. Boulder: National Center for Higher Education Management Systems, 1983.

Childers, Marie E. "What is Political About Bureaucratic-collegial Decision Making?" *The Review of Higher Education*, 5 (1981): 25–45.

Cicero, Marcus Tulius. *De divination*. Translated by W. A. Falconer. Cambridge: Harvard University Press, 1971.

Clarke, Ignatius F. "All Our Yesterdays," *Futures* 24 (1992): 251–261.

Coffey, Amanda and Paul Atkinson. *Making Sense of Qualitative Data*. Thousand Oaks: Sage, 1996.

Cohen, Michael D. and James G. March. *Leadership and Ambiguity: The American College President*. Boston: Harvard Business School Press, 1986.

Cohen, Michael D., James G. March, and Johan P. Olsen., J. P. A Garbage Can Model of Organizational Choice. *Administrative Science Quarterly*, 17 (1972): 1–25.

Council on Library Resources. *33rd Annual Report*. Washington DC: Council on Library Resources, 1989.

Council on Library Resources. *Automation and the Library of Congress*. Washington DC: U.S. Government Printing Office, 1963.

Courtney, Nancy. *Library 2.0 and Beyond: Innovative Technologies and Tomorrow's User*. Westport: Libraries Unlimited, 2007.

Crawford, Walt. *Being Analog: Creating Tomorrow's Libraries*. Chicago: American Library Association, 1999.

Crawford, Walt. "Where Have All the CD-ROMS Gone?" *American Libraries*, May 2001, 66–68.

Crawford, Walt and Michael Gorman. *Future Libraries: Dreams, Madness & Reality*. Chicago: American Library Association, 1995.

Crooks, Susan H. (1982). "Libraries in the Year 2000." In *Document delivery: Background papers commissioned by the Network Advisory Committee*, edited by Library of Congress Network Advisory Committee, 1–28. Washington DC: Library of Congress, 1982.

Crosbie, Michael J. and Damon D. Hickey. *When Change is Set in Stone: An Analysis of Seven Academic Libraries Designed by Perry Dean Rogers & Partners: Architects*. Chicago: Association of College and Research Libraries, 2001.

Cyert, Richard M. and James G. March. *A Behavioral Theory of the Firm*. Englewood Cliffs: Prentice Hall, 1963.

Dana, John C. *Changes in Library Methods in a Changing World*. Newark: The Public Library, 1927.

Darnton, Robert. *The Case For Books: Past, Present, and Future*. New York: PublicAffairs, 2009.

De Kock, M. G. "Using Scenarios in Planning a Digital Information Service." *South African Journal of Library & Information Service*, 66 (1998): 47–55.

Dewey, Melville. *Traveling Libraries*. Albany: University of the State of New York, 1901.

Dimaggio, Paul J. and Walter W. Powell. "The Iron Cage Revisited: Institutional Isomorphism and Collective Rationality in Organizational Fields." *American Sociological Review* 48 (1983): 147–160.

Discussion on Duplicating Processes. *Library Journal* 2 (1877): 33–34.

Drury, Francis K. W. "Labor-savers in Library Service." *Library Journal* 35 (1910): 538.

Dublin, Max. *Futurehype: The Tyranny of Prophecy.* New York: Dutton, 1991.

Edwards, Ward. "The Theory of Decision Making." *Psychological Bulletin* 51 (1954): 380–417.

Ehrenberg, Ronald G. "In Pursuit of University Wide Objectives." *Change*, 31 (1999): 28–31.

The Electronic Library. *New York Times.* December 21, 2004, A28.

Ellsworth, Ralph E. "Trends in Higher Education Affecting the College and University Library." *Library Trends* 1 (1952): 8–19.

Etzioni, Amatai. "Guidance Rules and Rational Decision Making." *Social Science Quarterly* 66 (1985): 755–769.

Evans, Christopher. *The Micro Millennium.* New York: Washington Square Press, 1979.

Fairchild, E. M. "Lantern Slides for Lectures in Library Work With Children." *Library Journal* 28 (1903): 156.

Fidler, Roger. "Life After 2001: Redefining Print Media in the Cyber Age." *Future of Print Media Journal, June 15, 1998.* http://www. futureprint.kent.edu/articles/fidler01.htm (accessed October 22, 2003).

Fincher, Cameron. "On the Rational Solution of Dominant Issues in Higher Education." *The Journal of Higher Education* 46 (1975): 491–505.

Fine Computer: A New Mechanical Device. *Public Libraries* 19 (1914): 260.

Finn, James D. *Automation in Educational Administration: Vending Machines in Schools and Colleges.* Washington DC: National Education Association, 1962.

Garnett, Richard. "Electric Light at the British Museum Reading Room." *Library Journal* 4 (1879): 444.

Giesecke, Joan. "Scenario Planning and Collection Development." *Journal of Library Administration* 28 (1999): 81–92.

Gleick, James. Faster: *The Acceleration of Just About Everything.* New York: Vintage, 2000.

Glenn, Jerome C. and Theodore J. Gordon. "Update on the State of the

Future." *The Futurist* 40 (2006): 21.

Glover, S. "Exotic Weeds and Cultural Change." *Current Anthropology* 47 (2006): 706.

Glueck, William F. and David M. Dennis. "Bureaucratic, Democratic and Environmental Approaches to Organizational Design." *Journal of Management Studies* 9 (1972): 196–205.

Google to Scan Books From Big Libraries. *USA Today*. December 14, 2009, ¶9. http://www.usatoday.com/tech/news/2004-12-14-google-books_x.htm (accessed September 20, 2010).

Gordon, Theodore J. "The Methods of Futures Research." *Annals of the American Academy of Political and Social Science* 522 (1992): 25–35.

Gore, Chris, Kate Murray, and Bill Richardson. *Strategic Decision Making*. New York: Cassell, 1992.

Gore, William J. and Fred S. Silander. "A Bibliographical Essay on Decision Making." *Administrative Science Quarterly* 4 (1959): 97–121.

Grammaphones in the Public Library as an Aid to Teaching Foreign Languages. *Library World* 19 (1917): 287–288.

Guba, Egon G. and Yvonna S. Lincoln. *Fourth Generation Evaluation*. Newbury Park: Sage, 1989.

Guest, Greg, Arwin Bunce, and Laura Johnson. "How Many Interviews Are Enough?: An Experiment With Data Saturation and Variability." *Field Methods* 18 (2006): 59–82.

Haas, John D. *Future Studies in the K–12 Curriculum*. Boulder: Social Science Education Consortium, 1988.

Hall, Crystal C., Lynn Ariss, and Alexander Todorov. "The Illusion of Knowledge: When More Information Reduces Accuracy and Increases Confidence." *Organizational Behavior and Human Decision Making Processes* 103 (2007): 277–290.

Hardesty, Larry, ed. *Books, Bytes, and Bridges*. Chicago: American Library Association, 2000.

Hardesty, Larry. Do we need academic libraries? January 21, 2000. http://www.ala.org/ala/mgrps/divs/acrl/publications/whitepapers/doweneedacademic.cfm (accessed September 21, 2010).

Hart, Paul. "Preventing Groupthink: Evaluating and Reforming Groups in Government." *Organizational Behavior and Human Decision Processes* 73 (1998): 306–326.

Hastings, Robin. "Journey to Library 2.0." *Library Journal* 132 (2007): 36–37.

Hawkins, Brian L. and Patricia Battin, Editors. *The Mirage of Continuity:*

Reconfiguring Academic Information Resources for the 21st Century. Washington DC: Council on Library and Information Resources, 1998.

Headicar, Bertie M. *The Library of the Future.* London: George Allen & Unwin, LTD, 1936.

Hedberg, Augustin. "Electronic Books Will Organize Your Life, Replace Your Library, and Fit In Your Pocket." *Money,* June 1989, 183–184.

Heiliger, Edward. "Florida Atlantic University: New Libraries on New Campuses." *College & Research Libraries* 25 (1964): 181–199.

Helgerson, Linda W. "CD-ROM: A Revolution in the Making." *Library High Tech* 4 (1986): 23–28.

Hellawell, David and Nick Hancock. "A Case Study of the Changing Role of the Academic Middle Manager in Higher Education: Between Hierarchical Control and Collegiality?" *Research Papers in Education* 16 (2001): 183–187.

Hernstein, Richard J. "Rational Choice Theory: Necessary But Not Sufficient." *American Psychologist* 45 (1990): 356–367.

Herring, Mark Y. *Fool's Gold: Why the Internet Is No Substitute For a Library.* Jefferson: McFarland, 2007.

Hickey, Thomas B. "The Journal in the Year 2000." *Wilson Library Bulletin* 56 (1981): 256–260.

Hirsch, Eric D. *Validity in Interpretation.* New Haven: Yale University Press, 1967.

Hickson, David J. "Decision Making at the Top of Organizations." *Annual Review of Sociology* 13 (1987): 165–192.

Hoy, Wayne K. and C. John Tartar. *Administrators Solving the Problems of Practice: Decision-making Concepts, Cases, and Consequences.* Boston: Allyn and Bacon, 1995.

Hsieh, Hsiu-Fang and Sarah E. Shannon. "Three Approaches to Qualitative Content Analysis." *Qualitative Health Research* 15 (2005): 1,277–1,288.

Huang, C. L., K. Wolfe, and J. McKissick. "Consumers' Willingness to Pay for Irradiated Poultry Products." *Journal of International Food & Agribusiness Marketing* 19 (2007): 77–95.

Huber, George P. "The Nature of Organizational Decision Making and the Design of Decision Support Systems." *MIS Quarterly* 5 (1981): 1–10.

Hughes, Carol A. (1992). "A Comparison of Perceptions of Campus Priorities: The 'Logical' Library in an Organized Anarchy." *The*

Journal of Academic Librarianship 18 (1992): 140–145.

Huwe, Terence K. "Surfing the Library 2.0 Wave." *Computers in Libraries*, 27 (2007): 36–38.

Iles, George. "The Work of Traveling Libraries." In *Traveling Libraries*, edited by Melville Dewey, 30–43. Albany: University of the State of New York, 1901.

Insel, Paul M. and Rudolph H. Moos. "Psychological Environments: Expanding the Scope of Human Ecology." *American Psychologist* 29 (1974), 179–188.

Ishisaka, Howard. "Human Ecology: The Interaction of Man With His Ecosystem. *Contemporary Education* 46 (1975): 114–118.

Jantsch, Erich. *Technological Forecasting in Perspective*. Paris, France: Organization for Economic Cooperation and Development, 1967.

Janzow, Laura M. *The Library Without the Walls*. New York: The H. W. Wilson Company, 1927.

Jeffries, R. "Good bye, Gutenberg!" *PC Magazine* 4 (1985): 95–98.

Jennings, Judson. T. "Extension of Library Service. In *The Library of Tomorrow: A Symposium*, edited by E. M. Danton, 78–86. Chicago: American Library Association, 1939.

Jones, Bryan D. *Politics and the Architecture of Choice: Bounded Rationality and Governance*. Chicago: University of Chicago Press, 2001.

Jurewicz, Lynn and Todd Cutler. *High Tech, High Touch: Library Customer Service Through Technology*. Chicago: American Library Association, 2003.

Kahneman, Daniel. "Judgment and Decision Making: A Personal View." *Psychological Science* 2 (1991): 142–145.

Kahneman, Daniel and Amos Tversky (1973). "On the Psychology of Prediction." *Psychological Review* 80 (1973): 237.

Kahney, Leander. "Microsoft: Paper is Dead." Wired News, August 30, 1999. http://www.wired.com/science/discoveries/news/1999/08/21499 (accessed September 20, 2010).

Kaplan, Sarah and Eric D. Beinhocker. "The Real Value of Strategic Planning." *MIT Sloan Management Review* 44 (2003): 71–76.

Karabell, Zachary. *A Visionary Nation: Four Centuries of American Dreams and What Lies Ahead*. New York: HarperCollins, 2001.

Kaser, David E. "Automation in Libraries of the Future." *Tennessee Librarian* 14 (1962): 79–84.

Katz, Richard N. "Competitive Strategies for Higher Education in the

Information Age." In *Dancing With the Devil: Information Technology and the New Competition in Higher Education*, edited by Richard N. Katz, 27–49. San Francisco: Jossey-Bass, 1999.

Keller, George. *Academic Strategy: The Management Revolution in American Higher Education*. Baltimore: Johns Hopkins University Press, 1983.

Kepner, Charles H. and Benjamin B. Tregoe. *The Rational Manager: A Systematic Approach to Problem Solving and Decision Making*. New York, NY: McGraw-Hill, 1965.

Kingdon, John W. *Agendas, Alternatives, and Public Policies*. New York: Longman, 1995.

Kountz, John. "Tomorrow's Libraries: More Than a Modular Telephone Jack, Less Than a Complete Revolution." *Library Hi Tech* 10 (1992): 39–50.

Kroeger, Alice B. "Instruction in Cataloging in Library Schools." *Library Journal* 32 (1907): 111.

Kurzweil, Ray. "The Future of Libraries Part 2: The End of Books." *Library Journal* 117 (1992): 140–141.

Kurzweil, Ray. "The Virtual Library." *Library Journal* 118 (1993): 54–55.

Lakoff, George and Marc Johnson. *Metaphors We Live By*. Chicago: University of Chicago, 1980.

Lambert, Steve and Suzanne Ropiequet, editors. *The New Papyrus: The Current and Future State of the Art*. Redmond: Microsoft Press, 1986.

Lancaster, F. Wilfred. *Toward Paperless Information Systems*. New York: Academic Press, 1978.

Lancaster, F. Wilfred. *Libraries and Librarians in an Age of Electronics*. Arlington: Information Resources Press, 1982.

Lancaster, F. Wilfred. "The Library Without Walls." Paper prepared for a meeting organized by the Public Library of Columbus & Franklin County and OCLC, Inc., held in Columbus, March 23–24, 1981.

Lancaster, F. Wilfrid, Laura S. Drasgow, and Ellen B. Marks. "The Changing Face of the Library: A Look at Libraries and Librarians in the Year 2001." *Collection Management* 3 (1979): 55–77.

Lancaster, F. Wilfrid, Laura S. Drasgow, and Ellen B. Marks. *The Impact of a Paperless Society on the Research Library of the Future*. Springfield: National Technical Information Service, U. S. Department of Commerce, 1980 (NTIS No. PB 80-204548).

Leimkuhler, Ferdinand F. and A. E. Neville. "The Uncertain Future of the Library." *Wilson Library Bulletin* 43 (1969): 30–38.

Lenzner, Robert and Stephen Johnson. "Seeing Things as They Really Are." *Forbes* 159 (1997): 122–128.

Lewis, David W. "A Strategy for Academic Libraries in the First Quarter of the 21st Century." *College & Research Libraries*, 68 (2007): 418–434.

Licklider, Joseph C. R. *Libraries of the future*. Cambridge: M.I.T. Press, 1965.

Lottman, Herbert R. "Frankfurt Book Fair, 1979." In *The Bowker Annual of Library & Book Trade Information,* 25th ed., edited by Filomena Simora. New York: R. R. Bowker Company, 1980.

Loye, David. *The Knowable Future: A Psychology of Forecasting and Prophecy*. New York: John Wiley & Sons, 1978.

Lucker, Jay. "Negotiating the Rocky Shoals: The Politics of Building a Library." In *Is the Library a Place?,* edited by Pamela Bixby, 23–27. Washington DC: Association of Research Libraries, 1991.

Lyon, David. *The Information Society: Issues and Illusions*. Cambridge: Polity Press, 1988.

Macpherson, Reynold J. S. "Escaping to Technology-based Distributed Faculty Development: A Case for Reforming Professional Development in a Knowledge Organization." *International Journal of Leadership in Education* 3 (2000): 275–291.

Maloney, Krisellen, Kristin Antelman, Kenning Arlitsch, and John Butler. "Future Leaders' Views on Organizational Culture." *College & Research Libraries* 71 (2010): 322–347.

Mansfield, B. "The Social Nature of Natural Childbirth." *Social Science & Medicine* 66 (2008): 1,084–1,094.

March, James G. "The 1978 Nobel Peace Prize in Economics." *Science, New Series* 202 (1978): 858–861.

March, James G. (1991). "How Decisions Happen in Organizations." *Human-Computer Interaction*, 6 (1991): 95–117.

March, James G. A Primer on Decision Making: How Decisions Happen. New York: *The Free Press*, 1994.

Markley, O. W. and Walter R. McCuan, Editors. *America Beyond 2001: Opposing Viewpoints*. San Diego: Greenhaven Press, 1996.

Marnet, Oliver. "History Repeats Itself: The Failure of Rational Choice Models in Corporate Governance." *Critical Perspectives on Accounting* 18 (2007): 191–210.

Marshall, Catherine and Gretchen B. Rossman. *Designing Qualitative Research*, 3rd ed. Thousand Oaks: Sage, 1999.

Martino, Joseph P. *Technological Forecasting for Decisionmaking*. New York: American Elsevier, 1972.

Martino, Joseph P. "Technological Forecasting: An Introduction." *The Futurist* 27 (1993): 13–16.

Masthead. Library Trends 1 (1952).

May, Matthew. "The Book Opens a New Chapter: Electronic Book." *Times*, April 13, 1989. *Custom Newspapers* database, InfoTrac-Gale, accessed August 24, 2010.

McConnell, Thomas R. "Faculty Government." In *Power and Authority: Transformation of Campus Governance*, edited by Harold L. Hodgkinson and L. Richard Meeth, 100. San Francisco: Jossey Bass, 1971.

McDonald, John. "No One Uses Them So Why Should We Keep Them?: Scenarios For Print Issue Retention." *Against the Grain* 15 (2003): 22–24.

McGregor, D. "The Major Determinants of the Prediction of Social Events." *Journal of Abnormal and Social Psychology* 33 (1938): 179–204.

McMurry, Robert N. "The Case for Benevolent Autocracy." *Harvard Business Review* 36 (1958): 82–90.

Mehnert, Robert B. "National Library of Medicine." In *The Bowker Annual of Library & Book Trade Information*, 24th ed., edited by Filomena Simora and Nada B. Glick. New York: R. R. Bowker Company, 1979.

Meister-Scheytt, Claudia and Tobias Scheytt. "The Complexity of Change in Universities." *Higher Education Quarterly* 59 (2005): 76–99.

Merriam, Sharan B. *Qualitative Research and Case Study Applications in Education*. 2nd ed. San Francisco: Jossey-Bass, 1998.

Metz, Paul. "The View From the University Library." *Change* 27 (1995): 28–33.

Milam, Carl H. "Experimentation." In *The Library of Tomorrow: A Symposium*, edited by Emily M. Danton, 47–59. Chicago: American Library Association, 1939.

Miles, Matthew B. and A. Michael Huberman. *Qualitative Data Analysis: An Expanded Sourcebook*, 2nd ed. Thousand Oaks: Sage Publications, 1994.

Miller, Tim. "Silver Platter: Dishing Up Data For Libraries." *Information Today*, June 1986, 23–39.

Mish, Frederick C., Editor. *Merriam-Webster's Collegiate Dictionary*.

10th ed. Springfield: Merriam-Webster, 1993.

Mitchell, Arnold, et al. *Handbook of Forecasting Techniques.* Menlo Park: Center for the Study of Social Policy, Stanford Research Institute, 1975.

Moldow, Susan. "Publish or Perish." *Newsweek*, June 26, 2000, 72.

Morris, Margaret F. "Experiences With a Library Network." *RQ* 9 (1969): 39–44.

Morrison, James L. "Using Futures Research in College and University Planning." Paper presented to the 1990 NCAIR Summer Drive-In Conference, August, 1990.

Morrison, James L., William L. Renfro, and Wayne I. Boucher. *Futures Research and the Strategic Planning Process: Implications for Higher Education.* Washington DC: Association for the Study of Higher Education, 1984.

"Mosaic Network Navigator Offered Free on the Internet." *Database Magazine* 17 (1994): 67.

"Moving Pictures in Library Work." *Wilson Library Bulletin* 6 (1910): 138–140.

Naisbitt, John. Megatrends: *Ten New Directions Transforming Our Lives.* New York: Warner Books, 1982.

Nardi, Bonnie A. and Vicki L. O'Day. *Information Ecologies: Using Technology With Heart.* Cambridge: MIT Press, 1999.

National Research Council. *Preparing for the Revolution: Information Technology and the Future of the Research University.* Washington DC: National Academies Press, 2002.

Naughton, John. *A Brief History of the Future: From Radio Days to Internet Years in a Lifetime.* Woodstock: Overlook Press, 2000.

Neal, James G. and Polley A. McClure. "Organizing Information Resources for Effective Management. In *Organizing and Managing Information Resources On Your Campus*, edited by Poley A. McClure, 29–44. San Francisco: Jossey-Bass, 2003.

Negropante, Nicholas. *Being Digital.* New York: Vintage Books, 1995.

Nicol, D. "Preface." In *Future Studies: An International Survey*, edited by J. McHale and M. C. McHale, iv. New York: United Nations Institute for Training and Research, 1976.

Norris, J. M. "Pawns or Professionals: The 21st Century Admissions Counselor." *Journal of College Admission* 189 (2005): 9–13.

OCLC Online Computer Library Center. *Libraries: How They Stack Up.* 2003. http://www.oclc.org/index/compare (accessed January

6, 2004).

O'Connor, Richard A. and Scott Bennett. "The Power of Place in Learning." *Planning for Higher Education* 33 (2005): 28–30.

O'Leary, Mick. "Ebook Scenarios." *Online* 25 (2001): 62–64.

O'Leary, Mick. "Ebook Scenarios Updated." *Online* 27 (2003): 59–60.

Olsen, Barbara J. and Carl F. Orgren. "Statewide Teletype Reference Service." *RQ* 15 (1976): 203–209.

Payne, John W. "The Scarecrow's Search: A Cognitive Psychologist's Perspective on Organizational Decision Making." In *Organizational Decision Making*, edited by Zur Shapira, 354–370. New York: Cambridge University Press, 1997.

Perlis, Alan J. (1962). "The Computer in the University. In *Management and the Computer of the Future*, edited by M. Greenberger, 180–217. Cambridge: M.I.T. Press, 1962.

Pfeffer, Jeffrey. *Managing with Power: Politics and Influence in Organizations*. Boston: Harvard Business School Press, 1992.

Phonograph Record Collection at St. Paul (Minn.) Library. *Library Journal* 45 (1920): 133.

Piggott, Sylvia. "The Virtual Library: Almost There." *Special Libraries* 84 (1993): 206–212.

Pin, Wan Wee. "Library 2.0: The New World Order." *Public Library Quarterly* 27 (2008): 244–246

Platt, John. R. "Where Will the Books Go?" *Horizon* 5 (1962): 42–47.

Player Piano Roles. *American Library Annual* 17 (1916): 95.

Plous, Scott. *The Psychology of Judgment and Decision Making*. Philadelphia: Temple University Press, 1993.

Plummer, Mary W. "Photograph Collection of Pratt Institute Free Library." *Library Journal* 24 (1899): 637.

Poole, Herbert. "Teletypewriters in Libraries: A Sate of the Art Report." *College & Research Libraries* 27 (1966): 283–286.

Powers, William. Hamlet's Blackberry: *A Practical Philosophy for Building a Good Life in the Digital Age*. New York: Harper, 2010.

Ranganathan, Shiyali R. *The Five Laws of Library Science*. London: Edward Goldston,1931.

Rawlins, William K. "Consensus in Decision-making Groups: A Conceptual History." In *Emergent Issues in Human Decision Making*, edited by Gerald M. Phillips and Julia T. Wood, 27–36. Carbondale: Southern Illinois University Press, 1984.

Rees, Alan M. "Librarians and Information Centers." *College & Research Libraries* 25 (1964): 200–204.

Rescher, Nicholas. *Predicting the Future: An Introduction to the Theory of Forecasting.* Albany: State University of New York, 1998.

Rider, Fremont. *The Scholar and the Future of the Research Library: A Problem and Its Solution.* New York: Hadham Press, 1944.

Rogers, Everett M. *Diffusion of Innovations*, 4th ed. New York: Free Press, 1995.

Rogers, Frank B. "The Development of MEDLARS." *Bulletin of the Medical Library Association* 52 (1964): 150–151.

Rogers, Michael. "Sony's Electronic Book: A New Library Format?" *Library Journal* 116 (1991): 26.

Rohrbach, Peter T. *FIND: Automation at the Library of Congress, The First Twenty-five Years and Beyond.* Washington DC: Library of Congress, 1985.

Roistacher, Richard C. "The Virtual Journal." *Computer Networks* 2 (1978): 18–24.

Rubin, Herbert J. and Irene S. Rubin. *Qualitative Interviewing: The Art of Hearing Data.* Thousand Oaks: Sage, 1995.

Salancik, Gerald R. and Jeffrey Pfeffer. "The Bases and Use of Power in Organizational Decision Making: The Case of a University." *Administrative Science Quarterly* 19 (1974): 453–473.

Sapp, Gregg and Ron Gilmour, "A Brief History of Academic Libraries: Predictions and Speculations From the Literature of the Profession—Part One, 1975 to 1989," *Portal: Libraries and the Academy* 2 (2002): 553–576.

Sardar, Ziauddin. *Rescuing All Our Futures: The Future of Future Studies.* Westport: Praeger, 1999.

Saunders, Peter G. "The Costs of Disability and the Incidence of Poverty." *Australian Journal of Social Issues* 42 (2007): 461–480.

Scepanski, Jordan M. "Forecasting, Forestalling, Fashioning: The Future of Academic Libraries and Librarians. In *Academic Libraries: Their Rationale and Role in American Higher Education*, edited by G. B. McCabe and R. J. Person, 167–175. Westport: Greenwood Press, 173.

Schaffner, Bradley L. "Electronic Resources: A Wolf in Sheep's Clothing?" *College & Research Libraries*, 62 (2001): 239–249.

Schmidt, Richard N. "Executive Decision Making." In *Current Issues and Emerging Concepts in Management*, edited by Paul M. Dauten,

100–109. New York, NY: Houghton Mifflin, 1962.

Schnaars, Steven P. *Megamistakes: Forecasting and the Myth of Rapid Technological Change*. New York: The Free Press, 1989.

Schniederjans, Marc J., Jamie L. Hamaker, and Ashlyn M. Schniederjans. *Information Technology Investment: Decision-making Methodology*. River Edge: World Scientific, 2004.

Schrage, Michael. "Good-bye, 'Dallas,' Hello, Videodiscs." *New York Magazine*, November 17, 2000, 38.

Schwab, John Christopher. "The Use of the Teleautograph at Yale University." *ALA Bulletin* 3 (1909): 371–372.

Schwalbe, Kathryn A. "A Study of the Relationship Between Investment in Information Technology and Institutional Outcomes in Higher Education." PhD diss., University of Minnesota, 1996.

Seidel, John and Udo Kelle. "Different Functions of Coding in the Analysis of Textual Data. In *Computer-aided Qualitative Data Analysis: Theory, Methods and Practice*, edited by Udo Kelle, 52–61. Thousand Oaks: Sage, 1995.

Seidman, Irving. *Interviewing as Qualitative Research: A Guide for Researchers in Education and the Social Sciences*. 2nd ed. New York: Teachers College Press, 1998.

Seiler, Lauren H. and Thomas T. Surprenant. "The Virtual Information Center: Scholars and Information in the Twenty-first Century." In *Libraries and the Future: Essays on the Library in the Twenty-first Century*, edited by F. Wilfred Lancaster, 157–180. New York: Haworth Press, 1993.

Sellers, Martin. "Moogle, Google, and Garbage Cans: The Impact of Technology on Decision Making. *International Journal of Leadership in Education* 8 (2005): 365–374.

Shapira, Zur. "Introduction and Overview." In *Organizational Decision making*, edited by Zur Shapira, 4. New York: Cambridge University Press, 1997.

Shera, Jesse H. "Tomorrow, and Tomorrow, and Tomorrow!" *ALA Bulletin* 33 (1939): 249, 278.

Sherden, William A. *The Fortune Sellers: The Big Business of Buying and Selling Predictions*. New York: John Wiley, 1998.

Shuman, Bruce A. *The Library of the Future: Alternative Scenarios for the Information Profession*. Englewood: Libraries Unlimited, 1989.

Silverman, David. *Doing Qualitative Research: A Practical Handbook*. 2nd ed. Thousand Oaks: Sage, 2005.

Simon, Herbert A. "Administrative Decision Making." *Public Administration Review* 25 (1965): 31–37.

Simon, Herbert A. *Administrative Behavior: A study of Decision-making Processes in Administrative Organization*. New York, NY: Free Press, 1976.

Slocum, Michael S. and Catherine O. Lundberg. "Technology Forecasting: From Emotional to Empirical." *Creativity and Innovation Management* 10 (2001): 139–152.

Slovic, Paul, Baruch Fischhoff, and Sarah Lichtenstein. Behavioral Decision Theory. *Annual Review of Psychology* 28 (1977): 1–39.

Slutsker, Gary and Jan Parr. "Waiting For New Hardware." *Forbes*, November 17, 1986, 262.

Smith, Eldred R. *The Librarian, the Scholar, and the Future of the Research Library*. New York: Greenwood, 1990.

Smith, Eldred R. "The Print Prison." *Library Journal* 117 (1992): 48–51.

Sommer, Robert, and Barbara Sommer. *A Practical Guide to Behavioral Research*. New York: Oxford University Press, 2002.

Sondak, Norman E. and Robert J. Schwartz. "The Paperless Journal." *Chemical Engineering Progress* 69 (1973): 82–83.

Soule, Charles C. *How to Plan a Library Building for Library Work*. Boston: The Boston Book Company, 1912.

Starr, Paul. "Transforming the Libraries: From Paper to Microfiche." *Change* 6 (1974): 34–40.

Stevens, Norman D. "A Popular History of Library Technology." In *Library Technology 1970–1990: Shaping the Library of the Future*, edited by Nancy M. Nelson, 1–14. Westport: Meckler, 1990.

Store, Ron and Wendy Way. "Teletypewriter Service for the Deaf." *The Unabashed Librarian* 31 (1979): 4.

Swingle, Walter T. "Utilization of Photographic Methods in Library Research Work." *ALA Bulletin* 10 (1916): 194–199.

Taylor-Powell, Ellen and Marcus Renner. *Analyzing Qualitative Data*. Madison: University of Wisconsin, 2003.

Tenopir, Carol. "What's Happening With CD-ROM." *Library Journal* 114 (1989): 50–51.

Thompson, I. "Collaboration in Technical Communication: A Qualitative Content Analysis of Journal Articles, 1990–1999." *IEEE Transactions On Professional Communication* 44 (2001): 161–173.

Thompson, James. *The End of Libraries*. London: Clive Bingley, 1982.

Thorin, Suzanne E. "Why Libraries?" *Research & Creative Activity* 23 (January 2001): ¶7. http://www.indiana.edu/~rcapub/v23n3/p03.html (accessed January 6, 2004).

Tocqueville, Alex de. *Democracy in America.* Translated by G. Lawrence. Chicago: Encyclopaedia Britannica, 1990.

Tversky, Amos. and Daniel Kahneman. "Rational Choice and the Framing of Decisions." *Journal of Business* 59 (1986): 251–278.

Tversky, Amos and Eldar Shafir. "The Disjunction Effect in Choice Under Uncertainty." *Psychological Science* 3 (1992): 305–309.

Uzanne, Octave. "The End of Books." *Scribner's Magazine Illustrated*, 16 (1894): 221–231.

Vig, Elizabeth K., Helene Starks, Janelle Taylor, Elizabeth Hopley, Kelly Fryer-Edwards (2007). "Surviving Surrogate Decision-making: What Helps and Hampers the Experience of Making Medical Decisions for Others." *Journal of General Internal Medicine* 22 (2007): 1,274–1,279.

Wallman, Sandra. "Introduction: Contemporary Futures." In *Contemporary Futures*, edited by Sandra Wallman, 1–18. New York: Routledge, 1992.

Watstein, Sarah B. "Scenario Planning for the Future of Reference: Five White Papers Posit the Future and Raise the Bar For Us All." *Reference Services Review* 31 (2003): 36–38.

Webb, William H. "Collection Development for the University and Large Research Library: More and More Versus Less and Less." In *Academic Libraries by the Year 2000*, edited by Herbert Poole, 139–151. New York: R. R. Bowker, 1977.

Weber, Max. *From Max Weber: Essays in Sociology*. Translated, edited, and with an introduction by Hans H. Gerth and C. Wright Mills. New York, NY: Oxford University Press, 1946.

Weber, Max. *The Theory of Social and Economic Organization*. Translated by Alexander M. Henderson and Talcott Parsons. New York: The Free Press, 1964.

Weiskel, Timothey C. "Libraries as Life-systems: Information, Entropy, and Coevolution on Campus." *College & Research Libraries* 47 (1986): 545–563.

Wheelright, Steven C. and Spyros G. Makridakis. *Forecasting Methods for Management*. New York: John Wiley, 1973.

Wheelwright, Philip E. *Heraclitus*. New York: Athenium, 1971.

White, Marilyn D. and Emily E. Marsh. "Content Analysis: A Flexible

Methodology." *Library Trends* 55 (2006): 22–45.

Wilson, Ian H. "Scenarios." In *Handbook of futures research*, edited by Jib Fowles, 225–247. Westport: Greenwood Press, 1978.

Winsor, Justin. "Telephones in Libraries." *Library Journal*, 2 (1877): 22.

Wisner, William H. *Whither the Postmodern Library?: Libraries, Technology, and Education in the Information Age*. Jefferson: McFarland, 2000.

Woike, Barbara A. Content Coding of Open-ended Responses. In *Handbook of Research Methods in Personality Psychology*, edited by R. W. Robins, R. C. Fraley, and R. F. Krueger, 292–307. New York: The Guilford Press, 2007.

The Women's College Library: The Present and the Future. Greensboro: Walter Clinton Jackson Library, 1939.

Wood, Michael T. "Power Relationships and Group Decision Making in Organizations." *Psychological Bulletin*, 79 (1973): 280–293.

Woodsworth, Anne. "The Model Research Library: Planning For the Future." *The Journal of Academic Librarianship* 15 (1989): 132–138.

Wooster, Harold. "Towards a Uniform Federal Report Numbering System and a Cuddly Microfiche Reader—Two Modest Proposals." *NMA Journal* 2 (1968): 63–69.

Wright, Alex. Glut: *Mastering Information Through the Ages*. Washington DC: Joseph Henry Press, 2007.

Wright, Ethel. C. "Use of the Victrola in the Story Hour." *Minnesota Public Library Commission Notes* 4 (1914): 126.

Wyndham, Miles D. A *History of the National Library of Medicine: The Nation's Treasury of Medical Knowledge*. Bethesda: U.S. Department of Health and Human Services, 1982.

S. David Mash

S. David Mash, a native Texan, graduated from the School of Library and Information Science at the University of North Texas. In addition to undergraduate and graduate work in psychology and theology, he is also a graduate of the higher education administration Ph.D. program at the University of South Carolina. He presently serves as the dean of library services at Lander University in Greenwood, South Carolina.

Decision Making in the Absence of Certainty

Research methodology, 65–82
Rider University, 20
Rogers, Everett M., 6
Rudolph Continuous Indexer, 7

S

Scenario development, 53–54
Scholarly Information Center, 16
Silander, Fred, 29
Silver Platter Information Services, 17
Simon, Herbert A., 41
The solution stream, 39, 91–100, 109
Space problems, 59, 103, 107
Stanford University, 32
Stereographs, 8
Streams of an organization, 65, 124
    the choice opportunities stream, 39
    the participant stream, 39, 66–82
    the problem stream, 38–39
    the solution stream, 39, 91–100, 109
"Sufficing," 32
"Surfing the Library 2.0 Wave," 23
Symbolic value, 90–91, 105, 106
Synchronous society, 60

T

"Talking books," 9
Technology and libraries, 7–12
Technology forecasts, see
    Forecasting, technological
Teleauthograph, 8
Teleology of progress, 22
Teletype, 8, 10
Temporal sorting, 101
Traveling libraries, 9
Trend extrapolation, 52–53
Triangle Research Libraries
    Network, 19

U

Ultrafax, 10
Universities
    as "organized anarchies," 37–38

redefined, 22
University of Bergen, 37
University of North Carolina, Chapel Hill, 57
University of Chicago, 12
University of Kansas, 21
University of Illinois. Center for Advanced Computation, 15
University of Illinois. Graduate School of Library Science, 1, 15–16
University of Michigan, 37
University of Minnesota, 19
University of New Mexico, 6
University of New York. Downstate Medical Center, 12
University of North Carolina, 8
University of Pennsylvania, 57
University of Pittsburgh, 51
University of Virginia, 113, 119
University of Windsor, 60
User considerations, 97
Uzanne, Octave, 12–13

V

Value congruence, 95–96
Value incongruence, 88–89
Victrola, 8
Videodisc, 17
"The Videodisc: Challenge and Opportunity for Publishers," 17
Virginia Tech University, 20, 105
Virtual journals, 15
Virtual libraries, 1, 19, 59

W

Web browser, 20
Western Reserve University, 12
Wright, Alex, 22

Y

Yale University, 8, 36, 59